CliffsNotes™

Death of a Salesman

By Jennifer L. Scheidt, M.A.

IN THIS BOOK

- Learn about the Life and Background of the Playwright
- Preview an Introduction to the Play
- Study a graphical Character Map
- Explore themes and literary devices in the Critical Commentaries
- Examine in-depth Character Analyses
- Enhance your understanding of the work with Critical Essays
- Reinforce what you learn with CliffsNotes Review
- Find additional information to further your study in CliffsNotes Resource Center and online at www.cliffsnotes.com

Wiley Publishing, Inc.

About the Playwright

Jennifer L. Scheidt received her M.A. from the University of Texas at San Antonio and is a full-time instructor at Palo Alto College in San Antonio, Texas, where she teaches various writing and literature courses.

Publisher's Acknowledgments

Editorial

Project Editor: Tracy Barr

Acquisitions Editor: Greg Tubach

Glossary Editors: The editors and staff at Webster's New World™ Dictionaries

Editorial Administrator: Michelle Hacker

Production

Indexer: York Production Services, Inc.

Proofreader: York Production Services, Inc.

Wiley Indianapolis Composition Services

CliffsNotes™ *Death of a Salesman*

Published by:
Wiley Publishing, Inc.
111 River Street
Hoboken, NJ 07030
www.wiley.com

Copyright © 2001 Wiley Publishing, Inc., Hoboken, NJ
Library of Congress Control Number: 00-107703
ISBN: 0-7645-8665-3

10 9 8 7 6 5 4
1O/RQ/RQ/QT/IN
Published by Wiley Publishing, Inc., Hoboken, NJ
Published simultaneously in Canada

No part of this publication may be reproduced, stored in a retrieval system, or transmitted in any form or by any means, electronic, mechanical, photocopying, recording, scanning, or otherwise, except as permitted under Sections 107 or 108 of the 1976 United States Copyright Act, without either the prior written permission of the Publisher, or authorization through payment of the appropriate per-copy fee to the Copyright Clearance Center, 222 Rosewood Drive, Danvers, MA 01923, 978-750-8400, fax 978-646-8600. Requests to the Publisher for permission should be addressed to the Legal Department, Wiley Publishing, Inc., 10475 Crosspoint Blvd., Indianapolis, IN 46256, 317-572-3447, fax 317-572-4447, or e-mail permcoordinator@wiley.com

For general information on our other products and services or to obtain technical support, please contact our Customer Care Department within the U.S. at 800-762-2974, outside the U.S. at 317-572-3993, or fax 317-572-4002.

Wiley also publishes its books in a variety of electronic formats. Some content that appears in print may not be available in electronic books.

Table of Contents

How to Use This Book

This CliffsNotes study guide on Arthur Miller's *Death of a Salesman* supplements the original literary work, giving you background information about the author, an introduction to the work, a graphical character map, critical commentaries, expanded glossaries, and a comprehensive index, all for you to use as an educational tool that will allow you to better understand *Death of a Salesman*. This study guide was written with the assumption that you have read *Death of a Salesman*. Reading a literary work doesn't mean that you immediately grasp the major themes and devices used by the author; this study guide will help supplement your reading to be sure you get all you can from Arthur Miller's *Death of a Salesman*. CliffsNotes Review tests your comprehension of the original text and reinforces learning with questions and answers, practice projects, and more. For further information on Arthur Miller and *Death of a Salesman*, check out the CliffsNotes Resource Center.

CliffsNotes provides the following icons to highlight essential elements of particular interest:

Reveals the underlying themes in the work.

Helps you to more easily relate to or discover the depth of a character.

Uncovers elements such as setting, atmosphere, mystery, passion, violence, irony, symbolism, tragedy, foreshadowing, and satire.

Enables you to appreciate the nuances of words and phrases.

Don't Miss Our Web Site

Discover classic literature as well as modern-day treasures by visiting the CliffsNotes Web site at www.cliffsnotes.com. You can obtain a quick download of a CliffsNotes title, purchase a title in print form, browse our catalog, or view online samples.

LIFE AND BACKGROUND OF THE PLAYWRIGHT

The following abbreviated biography of Arthur Miller is provided so that you might become more familiar with his life and the historical times that possibly influenced his writing. Read this Life and Background of the Author section and recall it when reading Miller's *Death of a Salesman,* thinking of any thematic relationship between Miller's novel and his life.

Personal Background

Arthur Miller was born in Harlem on October 17, 1915, the son of Polish immigrants, Isidore and Augusta Miller. Miller's father had established a successful clothing store upon coming to America, so the family enjoyed wealth; however, this prosperity ended with the Wall Street Crash of 1929. Financial hardship compelled the Miller family to move to Brooklyn in 1929.

Miller graduated from high school in New York in 1933. He applied to Cornell University and the University of Michigan, but both schools refused him admission. Miller worked a variety of odd jobs—including as a host of a radio program—before the University of Michigan accepted him. At school, he studied journalism, became the night editor of the *Michigan Daily*, and began experimenting with theater.

In addition to hosting a radio program, Miller held a variety of jobs during his early career. After he left the University of Michigan, Miller wrote plays for the Federal Theatre in 1939. The Federal Theatre provided work for unemployed writers, actors, directors, and designers. Congress closed the Federal Theatre late in 1939.

Career Highlights

Miller's prolific writing career spans a period of over 60 years. During this time, Miller has written 26 plays, a novel entitled *Focus* (1945), several travel journals, a collection of short stories entitled *I Don't Need You Anymore* (1967), and an autobiography entitled *Timebends: A Life* (1987). Miller's plays generally address social issues and center around an individual in a social dilemma or an individual at the mercy of society.

Miller's first play, *No Villain*, produced in 1936, explores Marxist theory and inner conflict through an individual facing ruin as a result of a strike. *Honors at Dawn* (1937) also centers around a strike and contrasting views of the economy but focuses on an individual's inability to express himself. *The Great Disobedience* (1938) makes a connection between the prison system and capitalism. *The Golden Years* (1940) tells the story of Cortes despoiling Mexico, as well as the effects of capitalism and fate on the individual.

Miller produced two radio plays in 1941: *The Pussycat and the Expert Plumber Who Was a Man*, and *William Ireland's Confession*. Miller's third radio play, *The Four Freedoms*, was produced in 1942.

The Man Who Had All the Luck (1944) revolves around a person who believes he has no control over his life but is instead the victim of chance. *All My Sons* (1947) explores the effect of past decisions on the present and future of the individual. *Death of a Salesman* (1949) addresses the loss of identity, as well as a man's inability to accept change within himself and society. *The Crucible* (1953) re-creates the Salem witch trials, focusing on paranoid hysteria as well as the individual's struggle to remain true to ideals and convictions.

A View from the Bridge (1955) details three people and their experiences in crime. *After the Fall* (1964) focuses on betrayal as a trait of humanity. *Incident at Vichy* (1964) confronts a person's struggle with guilt and responsibility. *The Price* (1968) tells the story of an individual confronted with free will and the burden of responsibility.

Fame (1970) tells the story of a famous playwright who is confronted but not recognized. *The American Clock* (1980) focuses on the Depression and its effects on the individual, while *Elegy for a Lady* (1982) addresses death and its effects on relationships. *Some Kind of Love Story* (1982) centers on society and the corruption of justice.

The Ride Down Mountain Morgan (1991) centers around a man who believes he can obtain everything he wants. *The Last Yankee* (1993) explores the changing needs of individuals and the resulting tension that arises within a marriage. *Broken Glass* (1994) tells the story of individuals using denial as a tool to escape pain. Miller also wrote the screenplay for the movie version of *The Crucible*, which was produced in 1996.

Honors and Awards

Miller has received numerous honors and awards throughout his career. Miller's accolades include the Michigan's Avery Hopwood Award, 1936 and 1937; the Theatre Guild's Bureau of New Plays Award, 1937; the New York Drama Critic's Circle Award, 1947; the Pulitzer Prize, 1949; the New York Drama Critic's Circle Award, 1949; the Antoinette Perry and Donaldson Awards, 1953; and the Gold Medal for Drama by the National Institutes of Arts and Letters, 1959. Miller was also elected president of PEN (Poets, Essayists, and Novelists) in 1965.

Miller died on February 10, 2005, of heart failure. He was 89 years old.

INTRODUCTION TO THE PLAY

The following Introduction section is provided solely as an educational tool and is not meant to replace the experience of your reading the novel. Read the Introduction and A Brief Synopsis to enhance your understanding of the novel and to prepare yourself for the critical thinking that should take place whenever you read any work of fiction or nonfiction. Keep the List of Characters and Character Map at hand so that as you read the original literary work, if you encounter a character about whom you're uncertain, you can refer to the List of Characters and Character Map to refresh your memory.

Introduction

Arthur Miller's play *Death of a Salesman* addresses loss of identity and a man's inability to accept change within himself and society. The play is a montage of memories, dreams, confrontations, and arguments, all of which make up the last 24 hours of Willy Loman's life. The play concludes with Willy's suicide and subsequent funeral.

Miller uses the Loman family—Willy, Linda, Biff, and Happy—to construct a self-perpetuating cycle of denial, contradiction, and order versus disorder. Willy had an affair over 15 years earlier than the real time within the play, and Miller focuses on the affair and its aftermath to reveal how individuals can be defined by a single event and their subsequent attempts to disguise or eradicate the event. For example, prior to discovering the affair, Willy's son Biff adored Willy, believed all Willy's stories, and even subscribed to Willy's philosophy that anything is possible as long as a person is "well-liked." The realization that Willy is unfaithful to Linda forces Biff to reevaluate Willy and Willy's perception of the world. Biff realizes that Willy has created a false image of himself for his family, society, and even for himself.

Willy is not an invincible father or a loyal husband or a fantastically successful salesman like he wants everyone to believe. He is self-centered. He fails to appreciate his wife. And he cannot acknowledge the fact that he is only marginally successful. Hence, Willy fantasizes about lost opportunities for wealth, fame, and notoriety. Even so, it would be incorrect to state that Miller solely criticizes Willy. Instead, Miller demonstrates how one individual can create a self-perpetuating cycle that expands to include other individuals. This is certainly the case within the Loman family. Until the end of the play, Willy effectively blocks the affair out of his memory and commits himself to a life of denial. He cannot remember what happened, so naturally he does not understand why his relationship with Biff has changed. Willy wants Biff's affection and adoration as before, but instead the two constantly argue. Willy vacillates, sometimes criticizing Biff's laziness and ineptitude, other times praising his physical abilities and ambition.

Linda and Happy are also drawn into the cycle of denial. Linda is aware of Willy's habit of reconstructing reality; however, she also recognizes that Willy may not be able to accept reality, as shown through his numerous suicide attempts prior to the beginning of the play. As a result, Linda chooses to protect Willy's illusions by treating them as truth, even if she must ignore reality or alienate her children in doing so. Happy is also a product of Willy's philosophy. Like Willy, he manipulates the truth to create a more favorable reality for himself. For example, when Happy tells everyone that he is the assistant buyer, even though he is only the assistant to the assistant, he proves that he has incorporated Willy's practice of editing facts.

Miller based Willy's character on his uncles, Manny Newman and Lee Balsam, who were salesmen. Miller saw his uncles as independent explorers, charting new territories across America. It is noteworthy that Miller does not disclose what type of salesman Willy is. Rather than drawing the audience's attention to "what" Willy sells, Miller chooses to focus on the fact that Willy is a "salesman." As a result, Miller expands the import of Willy's situation. Willy is an explorer—conqueror of the New England territory—and a dreamer, and this allows the audience to connect with him because everyone has aspirations, dreams, and goals.

Willy's despair results from his failure to achieve his American dream of success. At one point, Willy was a moderately successful salesman opening new territory in New England, and Biff and Happy viewed him as a model father. Once Biff discovers the affair, however, he loses respect for Willy as well as his own motivation to succeed. As Willy grows older, making sales is more difficult for him, so he attempts to draw on past success by reliving old memories. Willy loses the ability to distinguish reality from fantasy, and this behavior alienates him from others, thereby diminishing his ability to survive in the present. As the play progresses, Willy's life becomes more disordered, and he is forced to withdraw almost completely to the past, where order exists because he can reconstruct events or relive old memories.

The play continues to affect audiences because it allows them to hold a mirror up to themselves. Willy's self-deprecation, sense of failure, and overwhelming regret are emotions that an audience can relate to because everyone has experienced them at one time or another. Although most do not commit suicide in the face of adversity, people connect with Willy because he is a man driven to extreme action. An audience may react with sympathy toward Willy because he believes he is left with no other alternative but to commit suicide. On the other hand, an audience may react with disgust and anger toward Willy, believing he has deserted his family and taken the easy way out.

Either way, individuals continue to react to *Death of a Salesman* because Willy's situation is not unique: He made a mistake—one that irrevocably changed his relationship with the people he loves most—and when all of his attempts to eradicate his mistake fail, he makes one grand attempt to correct the mistake. Willy vehemently denies Biff's claim that they are both common, ordinary people, but ironically, it is the universality of the play that makes it so enduring. Biff's statement, "I'm a dime a dozen, and so are you" is true after all.

A Brief Synopsis

Death of a Salesman takes place in New York and Boston. The action begins in the home of Willy Loman, an aging salesman who has just returned from a road trip. Willy is having difficulty remembering events, as well as distinguishing the present from his memories of the past. His wife, Linda, suggests that he request a job in New York rather than travel each week. Linda and Willy argue about their oldest son Biff.

Biff and his brother, Happy, overhear Willy talking to himself. Biff learns that Willy is usually talking to him (Biff) during these private reveries. Biff and Happy discuss women and the future. Both are dissatisfied with their jobs: Biff is discontent working for someone else, and Happy cannot be promoted until the merchandise manager dies. They contemplate buying a ranch and working together.

At this point, Willy relives several scenes from his past, including the time when, during high school, Biff admits to stealing a football and promises to throw a pass for Willy during the game. Willy also remembers his old dream of the boys visiting him in Boston during a road trip. Finally in his reverie, he relives the time that Bernard, son of the next-door neighbor Charley, informs Willy that Biff is failing math and will not graduate unless his scores improve. In this last scene, Willy listens but dismisses the important news because Biff is "well-liked," and Bernard is not.

Willy remembers a conversation with Linda in which he inflates his earnings but is then forced to admit he exaggerated when Linda calculates his commission. Willy recalls complaining about his appearance and remembers Linda assuring him that he is attractive. At this point, Willy's memories begin to blend together. While he is reliving his conversation with Linda, he begins to remember his conversation with the Woman (a woman with whom he had an affair). He is unable to separate memories of Linda from the Woman.

The play continues in the present with his neighbor Charley coming over to play cards. However, Uncle Ben appears to Willy while he is playing cards with Charley, and Willy relives an old conversation with Ben while simultaneously talking with Charley. As a result, Willy becomes confused by the two different "discussions" he is having—one in the present, one in the past—and he accuses Charley of cheating. After Charley leaves, Willy relives Ben's visit and asks Ben for advice because he feels insecure since he did not really know his own father. Willy also remembers instructing Biff and Happy to steal some supplies from the construction site in order to remodel the porch so that he can impress Ben.

The play once again returns to the present, in which Biff and Happy talk with Linda about Willy. Biff and Happy learn that Willy is on straight commission and has been borrowing money from Charley in order to pay bills. Linda criticizes her sons for abandoning their father in order to pursue their own selfish desires, and she gives Biff a choice: Respect your father or do not come home. Biff decides to stay in New York, but he reminds Linda that Willy threw him out of the house. He also tells Linda that Willy is a "fake." It is at this point that Linda informs her sons that Willy is suicidal.

Willy overhears his wife and sons talking, and he and Biff argue. When Happy describes Biff's plan to open his own business, Willy directs Biff on what to do during his interview with Bill Oliver. Willy remembers Biff's football games. Before Linda and Willy go to bed, Linda questions Willy: She wants to know what Biff is holding against him, but Willy refuses to answer. Biff removes the rubber tubing Willy hid behind the heater.

The next morning Willy prepares to visit his boss Howard to ask him for a job in New York. During the meeting, Howard informs Willy that there are no positions available in New York. Willy reminds Howard that he named him, and he was a very successful salesman when he worked for Howard's father. Howard remains impassive and instead fires him.

Upon being fired, Willy begins freefalling into his memories of the past. Willy recalls Ben's visit once again. This time, Willy asks for advice because things are not going as he planned. He remembers Ben offering him a job in Alaska. He accepts, but Linda intervenes and reminds him of Dave Singleman. Willy shifts from his memory of Ben to Biff's last football game. Willy recalls Charley pretending he is unaware of

Biff's game, and this infuriates Willy. Willy's daydream ends when he arrives at Charley's office.

Bernard is waiting for Charley in his office. Willy and Bernard discuss Biff and consider possible reasons for his lack of motivation and success. Bernard says Biff changed right after high school when he visited Willy in Boston. Bernard questions Willy about what happened when Biff went to visit him. Willy becomes defensive. Bernard is on his way to present a case before the Supreme Court. Bernard's success both pleases and upsets Willy. Charley gives Willy money for his insurance payment and offers him a job, an offer that Willy refuses.

At a restaurant where Willy, Biff, and Happy are to meet, Happy flirts with a young prostitute, and Biff is upset because Oliver did not remember him. Then Biff realizes that he was never a salesman for Oliver; instead, he was a shipping clerk. Willy tells his sons that he has been fired. Biff attempts to explain what happened with Oliver (after seeing Oliver, Biff sneaked back into his office and stole Oliver's pen); however, Willy is reliving the past, recalling Bernard informing Linda that Biff has failed math and will not graduate. Willy then remembers Bernard telling her Biff has taken a train to Boston.

Willy relives the time when Biff finds out about Willy's affair with the Woman: Biff comes to Willy's hotel room in Boston to tell Willy that he will not graduate unless Willy can convince Mr. Birnbaum to pass him. Willy recalls his own desperate attempts to hide the Woman in the bathroom. When the Woman comes out of the bathroom with Biff in the room, Willy's plan to conceal the affair is ruined. Willy's final memory is of Biff calling him a "fake" before walking out the door.

The play continues in the present when Stanley reappears, and Willy realizes he is actually still in the restaurant. Willy returns home and begins building a garden, even though it is night. Linda throws Happy and Biff out of the house. Ben appears to Willy while he is planting seeds. At this point, Willy does not remember a previous conversation with Ben, as he does several times earlier in the play. Instead, he and Ben discuss his plan to commit suicide. Willy and Ben converse in the present, but they are talking about the future. Ben warns Willy that the insurance company might refuse to pay a settlement and Biff might never forgive him.

Biff approaches Willy in the garden to tell him he is leaving home for good. Biff and Willy argue, and Biff confronts Willy with the rubber hose, saying he will not pity him if he commits suicide. According to

Biff, the Lomans have never been truthful with one another or themselves. Biff believes that he and Willy are ordinary people who can easily be replaced. Biff and Willy reconcile. Ben reappears to Willy and reminds him of the insurance policy. Willy drives away. The Lomans, Charley, and Bernard gather at Willy's grave.

List of Characters

Willy Loman   An aging salesman. He suffers from depression and anxiety as a result of his dissipating career, his estranged relationship with his oldest son, Biff, and his guilt over an extramarital affair. As the play progresses, Willy loses the ability to distinguish between the present and his memories of the past.

Linda Loman   Willy Loman's wife. She is Willy's champion and takes it upon herself to reconcile her family. She will protect Willy at all costs, even if she must perpetuate his fantasies and deny his suicidal behavior.

Biff Loman   The Lomans' older son. Biff has been estranged from Willy for over 15 years, during which time he has not been able to hold a steady job. Biff is the only member of the family who knows about Willy's affair, and he resents his father bitterly.

Happy Loman   The Lomans' younger son. Happy is a womanizer driven by his sexuality. He works as an assistant but exaggerates his position and his authority.

Uncle Ben   Willy's older brother. He made a fortune in the African jungle by the time he was 21 years old. He once offered Willy a job in Alaska. Ben appears in the play only in Willy's memories and fantasies.

Charley   A long-time acquaintance of the Lomans. Charley supplies Willy with a weekly loan once Willy is put on straight commission, and he repeatedly offers him a job. Charlie is a true friend to Willy, even though Willy is jealous of him. Charley appears in Willy's memories, as well as in the actions of the present.

Bernard   Charley's son. He provided Biff with answers while they were in high school and attempted to help Biff study so that he would graduate, even though Willy and Biff would criticize him. He is a successful lawyer. Bernard appears in Willy's memories, as well as in the present.

The Woman   Willy's former lover, with whom he had an affair many years ago in Boston. Biff discovered the affair when she came out of the bathroom while he was in the room. She appears only in Willy's memories and fantasies; however, as the play progresses, Willy has difficulty distinguishing between his memories of the Woman and his memories of Linda.

Howard Wagner   Willy's current boss. He put Willy on straight commission prior to the play's beginning, and later he fires him. Howard is a businessman, unaffected by the facts that Willy worked for his father and named him as a child.

Jenny   Charley's secretary.

Stanley   A waiter.

Miss Forsythe and Letta   Young prostitutes.

Character Map

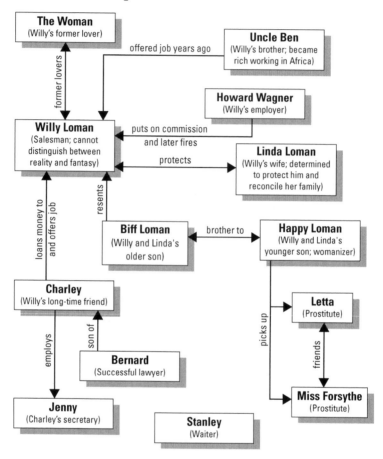

The Woman
(Willy's former lover)

Uncle Ben
(Willy's brother; became rich working in Africa)

offered job years ago

former lovers

Howard Wagner
(Willy's employer)

Willy Loman
(Salesman; cannot distinguish between reality and fantasy)

puts on commission and later fires

protects

Linda Loman
(Willy's wife; determined to protect him and reconcile her family)

loans money to and offers job

resents

Biff Loman
(Willy and Linda's older son)

brother to

Happy Loman
(Willy and Linda's younger son; womanizer)

Charley
(Willy's long-time friend)

employs

son of

picks up

Letta
(Prostitute)

friends

Bernard
(Successful lawyer)

Jenny
(Charley's secretary)

Stanley
(Waiter)

Miss Forsythe
(Prostitute)

CRITICAL COMMENTARIES

The sections that follow provide great tools for supplementing your reading of *Death of a Salesman*. First, in order to enhance your understanding of and enjoyment from reading, we provide quick summaries in case you have difficulty when you read the original literary work. Each summary is followed by commentary: literary devices, character analyses, themes, and so on. Keep in mind that the interpretations here are solely those of the author of this study guide and are used to jumpstart your thinking about the work. No single interpretation of a complex work like *Death of a Salesman* is infallible or exhaustive, and you'll likely find that you interpret portions of the work differently from the author of this study guide. Read the original work and determine your own interpretations, referring to these Notes for supplemental meanings only.

Act I—Scene 1

Summary

Death of a Salesman begins in the home of Willy Loman. Willy returns home exhausted from his latest sales excursion. He worries because he is having difficulty remembering events, as well as staying focused on the present. His wife, Linda, reassures him that he is only suffering from mental fatigue. Linda suggests that Willy should request a New York assignment rather than travel each week. At first Willy hesitates, complaining that his boss Howard does not respect his contributions to the company and might not listen to him, but Linda encourages Willy to tell Howard of his accomplishments. Willy decides to talk to Howard in the morning.

Willy and Linda argue about their son Biff. Willy calls Biff a "lazy bum," but Linda defends Biff on the premise that he is still trying to "find himself." Willy then contradicts his previous statement by saying that Biff is not lazy, and he decides to get Biff a job as a salesman. Willy drifts back into the past, remembering how everyone admired Biff when he was in high school. He comes out of his reverie and assures Linda that he is fine. He announces that he will no longer argue with Biff about his job. Linda suggests a picnic lunch, and Willy realizes that, all day, he thought he was driving the 1928 Chevy rather than the Studebaker.

Commentary

Theme

In Act I, Scene 1, Miller introduces the three major themes of *Death of a Salesman*: denial, contradiction, and order versus disorder. When Willy returns home early from a sales trip, Linda casually asks if he wrecked the car. Linda's question and Willy's annoyed response suggest that this conversation has happened before. He does not make excuses for himself but openly admits that he could not concentrate on his driving. In fact, several times, he forgot that he *was* driving. Willy realizes something is wrong with him, and he is exhausted both physically and mentally.

Scene 1 establishes the nature of the relationship between Willy and Linda. Although Willy states exactly what happened, Linda provides him with opportunities to deny that anything is wrong with him. In this way, she attempts to protect him from seeing his own short-comings. She suggests the faulty steering on the Studebaker, as well as Willy's glasses, as possible reasons why he cannot drive properly. Linda continues to support Willy, offering him excuses for his own behavior, as well as Biff's inability to maintain a steady job. In general, Willy takes Linda for granted and does not appreciate her, except in rare moments of clarity, such as at the end of Scene 1 when he asks if she is worried about him. During the majority of the play, Willy freely criticizes Linda and her opinion, unless they are alone together.

As the scene progresses, Willy struggles to reconcile memories from the past with the events of the present. According to Willy, the glory of past events should be precursors to the reality of the present. In other words, because he recollects such wonderful memories of order and success, these qualities should still exist for him in the present. For example, Willy believes he should be recognized and respected at work because he established the company throughout New England and named his own boss. He is not respected, however, because he has lost the ability to sell merchandise effectively. Things that Willy considers meaningful, such as past sales records and prior friendships, mean nothing in his current world, which is governed by the bottom line.

These contradictions are not inconsistencies in Willy's outlook, but rather a consistent part of his character. He customizes information, facts, and memories to fit his ideal perception of the world. When someone disagrees with Willy, he is insulted and becomes angry. He is tired of "always being contradicted." His son Biff is the character that "contradicts" him the most throughout the play. Willy criticizes Biff because he feels his son is wasting his life working on a farm in Texas, but Linda defends Biff because he is still "finding himself." Willy sees Biff's instability as a sign of laziness and lack of character; however, Willy's opinion of Biff changes as a result of his memories of Biff in high school. At the beginning of the conversation, he labeled Biff "a lazy bum," but later in the same conversation, Willy contradicts himself and describes Biff as a "hard worker." Willy believes Biff's popularity and success in high school make it impossible for Biff to be a disappointment now. He projects his past memories of Biff onto the present, convincing himself that his son will have the same effect on people now—as a salesman or a hired hand on a farm—that he did as a football player in high school. In other words, his son's situation is too difficult to acknowledge, so Willy creates an alternative reality that is much more palatable, denying the facts of the situation. In this way, Willy creates order from disorder because he manipulates facts to produce a better alternative.

Glossary

(Here and in the following glossary sections, difficult words and phrases, as well as allusions and historical references, are explained.)

tired to the death an expression meaning exhausted. Here, the phrase can also be interpreted literally because Willy has attempted suicide several times and is planning to try again.

undercurrent an underlying tendency, opinion, etc., usually one that is kept hidden and not expressed openly.

massacre to kill indiscriminately and mercilessly and in large numbers.

simonize to wax and polish a car.

Act I—Scene 2

Summary

Scene 2 begins in the boys' bedroom. Willy's sons, Biff and Happy, overhear him. Happy tells Biff that Willy has started talking to himself nearly all of the time. According to Happy, Willy is usually talking to Biff during his private reveries. The boys reminisce about old times and women. Biff explains that he has returned home because he is dissatisfied with his job and future prospects. Because Biff enjoys outdoor labor, working on the farm is ideal; however, Biff is discontent toiling for someone else. Biff dreams of owning his own ranch and working it with Happy. He contemplates asking Bill Oliver for financial support but is hesitant because he is afraid Bill will remember that he stole some basketballs from him as a teenager.

Happy becomes enthusiastic listening to Biff talk about the ranch and the possibility of working together. Although Happy has obtained all of the material things he desires—an apartment, a car, and a seemingly unending supply of women—he is also dissatisfied with his current lifestyle. He cannot be promoted until the merchandise manager leaves or dies, and he realizes that if he is promoted, he will be too busy worrying about obtaining more money and material goods to enjoy what he has.

Commentary

Scene 2 is important because it is the first time that the audience encounters Willy's sons firsthand. Now the audience has an opportunity to determine if Willy's opinion of Biff is justified.

Character Insight

Biff has changed a great deal from the time he was in high school when he thought anything was possible. Happy believes that he is more like Biff used to be than Biff himself because Happy's own actions stem from the belief that all things are possible and all goals are obtainable. Biff is no longer governed by these beliefs. In fact, Biff is overwhelmed by his own contradictory desires: He enjoys working outside on a farm, but when spring comes, he becomes impatient and feels the need to return to New York and "make something of himself." Biff's instability stems not only from his inability to maintain a steady job but his conflicting emotions for his father. Biff resents Willy's antagonism toward him, but he is also driven by a desire to please his father—a desire that he denies and hides from himself.

Biff is horrified by Happy's report of Willy's mumblings and imagined conversations. Biff hints that his father is troubled because of "other things"—namely Willy's affair—besides the fact that Biff is working as a lowly farmhand. On one hand, Biff feels that Willy's conduct is a manifestation of well-deserved guilt. On the other hand, he is disturbed to learn that Willy talks to him or about him during his reveries. Biff denies responsibility for his father's condition, but he is forced to acknowledge that he is linked to his father's guilt and irrational actions.

Biff attempts to establish order in his life by encouraging Happy to join him in Texas. Both of the boys have difficulty dealing with authority. According to Biff, "we weren't brought up to grub for money. I don't know how to do it." Therefore, Biff believes owning their own business would be the ideal job for both of them.

Character Insight

Biff knows what he needs in order to be content; Happy however, is incapable of finding contentment. He is a man driven by sexuality and a need for power. He has obtained material desires—an apartment, a car, and lots of women—but he cannot acquire peace. He targets women connected to his superiors and "ruins" them in order to prove to himself that he can. Although he is forced to endure working for individuals he feels are incompetent, he exacts revenge by stealing their women and "spoiling" them, thus forcing disorder into the order of his superiors.

Glossary

like   here the meaning is closer to likeable, having qualities that inspire liking; easy to like because attractive, pleasant, genial, and so on.

Act I–Scene 3

Summary

Scene 3 shifts back in time. Willy is actually in the kitchen, drinking a glass of milk; however, the action that he observes is in the past. Willy coaches Biff and Happy as they polish the old 1928 Chevy. He also surprises them with a punching bag. Happy mentions he is losing weight and asks if Willy has noticed. Biff shows Willy his new football and admits that he stole the ball from the school locker room. Willy disapproves and instructs Biff to return the ball, but then he defends Biff's action and praises his "initiative." Biff is nervous about the upcoming football game but promises to make a touchdown for Willy, even though he has been instructed to pass the ball. Willy is pleased and excited at the thought of telling everyone in Boston about the game.

Willy tells the boys about his recent trip to Providence, Waterbury, Boston, Portland, and Bangor. He shares a secret plan of owning a business so he will no longer have to travel. Willy also promises to take the boys with him on business trips during the summer. He imagines a grand entrance with Biff and Happy carrying his sample cases into the stores.

Commentary

Scene 3 is the first scene that takes place entirely in the past. This is important because the audience is observing the events as Willy remembers them. This scene is one of Willy's cherished memories because, in it, his children idealize him. Everything that Willy says or does is perfect, and he is an authority figure within the scene, instructing the boys on the proper technique to polish the car. He also plans to trim the tree branch over the house. This job is a pleasure because Willy and the boys delight in manual labor. The punching bag is the ideal gift because it represents the physical strength and dominance that Willy and the boys achieve through physical labor.

Scene 3 presents the audience with the first example of tension between Biff and Happy. This is an example of disorder even in Willy's orderly memories. Happy reveals that Biff has stolen a football. Willy immediately disapproves; however, he defends Biff when Happy criticizes him. Biff's action reflects his own struggle for order within his life. He steals the ball to practice so that he can play well during the Ebbet's Field game. His goal is to please Willy, but he goes about it the wrong way. The fact that Willy reprimands him and then praises him for stealing only leads to further confusion and disorder later in Biff's life. When Willy sanctions Biff's theft, he emphasizes the idea that it is permissible to break the rules to get ahead. Furthermore, Willy reinforces the notion that Biff is immune to boundaries that bind other members of society.

Glossary

insinuate to introduce or work into gradually, indirectly, and artfully.

immerse to absorb deeply; engross.

incipient in the first stage of existence; just beginning to exist or to come to notice.

initiative the action of taking the first step or move; responsibility for beginning or originating.

open sesame any unfailing means of gaining admission or achieving some other end; these words were spoken to open the door of the thieves' den in the story of Ali Baba in *The Arabian Nights*.

Act I—Scene 4

Summary

Scene 4 is also set in the past and continues with Willy's reverie in the kitchen. Bernard enters and asks Biff why he has not come over to study with him as planned. Bernard informs Willy that Biff will fail math and not graduate unless he begins to prepare for his exams. Willy and the boys ridicule Bernard. After Bernard leaves, Willy criticizes him and guarantees that Biff and Happy will be more successful than Bernard because they both have attractive physical features. Biff then tells Willy that Bernard is "liked, but he is not well-liked."

Commentary

The description of Biff's theft in Scene 3 lets the audience know that Biff is not the perfect person Willy might hope for him to be. Scene 4 is significant because it reveals that Biff has serious problems that may negatively impact his future. Although Willy teases Bernard, he does react responsibly to the news that Biff is in danger of failing math, as well as not graduating. Willy tells Biff to study, but he revels in the fact that his boys are superior in strength and popularity to everyone else. Their prowess functions as an extension of Willy, for he considers himself greater because of his children's abilities. They are "well liked," and therefore Willy is too.

The fact that Biff and Happy obviously outdo Bernard is significant because Willy has always felt threatened by and jealous of Bernard's father, Charley. Even though Willy instructs Biff to study, he does not emphasize the consequences if Biff fails, but instead stresses the fact that Bernard is not "well-liked." Willy denies that Biff could fail, so he does not communicate the possibility of failure to his son. Once again, Willy reinforces the idea that Biff is not answerable to the same social boundaries as others. Willy and his boys can achieve order and success in their lives so long as they follow their own rules.

Glossary

anemia   a condition in which there is a reduction of the number, or volume, of red blood corpuscles or of the total amount of hemoglobin in the bloodstream, resulting in paleness, generalized weakness.

Adonis   any very handsome young man.

Act I—Scene 5

Summary

Scene 5 continues in the past where Scene 4 ended. Linda enters the kitchen carrying a basket of laundry. Biff orders Happy and his friends, who are waiting down in the cellar, to help with the chores. Some hang laundry; others sweep out the furnace room. Linda and Willy are left alone and begin discussing his earnings from the trip to New England. Willy exaggerates his sales, telling Linda that he sold $1,200, but when she calculates his commission, Willy is forced to admit that he only sold $200. Linda recites an itemized list of bills that exceeds his $70 commission by approximately $50. Willy becomes agitated and refuses to pay for the carburetor for the Chevy because he considers the car worthless, even though he praised the car at the beginning of the scene.

Willy declares that he will be successful in Hartford because he is "well-liked," but he immediately follows that statement by saying that people do not respond well to him. Willy says that he talks and jokes too much, and that no one takes him seriously because of his appearance. Linda assures him that she finds him attractive and that his children love and respect him. Linda's comments encourage Willy, and he declares his affection for her. In the background, a woman's laughter can be heard, and a faint outline of a woman dressing becomes visible.

Commentary

Scene 5 is significant because it is the first time that Willy's manipulation of reality occurs in front of the audience. Although the scene continues in the past, picking up in the kitchen where Scene 4 left off, the audience is given the opportunity to observe Willy's tendency to exaggerate and deny reality. He is not satisfied with his earnings, or modicum of success, so he reinvents his success by exaggerating his sales to Linda. It is only when Linda confronts him with the numbers that he is forced to admit his true commission. Once Linda knows the truth, Willy can no longer pretend about his success, so he becomes argumentative and begins to contradict prior statements. For example, Willy's assertion that Chevrolet is "the greatest car ever built," is immediately revoked once his exaggeration is revealed. Criticism of the car is just one example of Willy's need to bring order to his life by passing judgment and thus appearing as an authority on something, or anything.

Character Insight

Willy's contradictions throughout the scene reveal his own inability to accept the truth about himself and the reality of the world he lives in. He knows that people criticize him because of his demeanor, and he realizes that people are no longer receptive to him. The fact that Willy acknowledges these things demonstrates that he knows the reality of the situation; however, his immediate contradictions prove his inability to accept the way things are. He denies his own failure as a salesman, along with his inability to be "well-liked," because they are too painful. It is much easier for him to invent a reality in which he is successful, thereby creating order in a disordered existence.

Glossary

crack to hit or strike with a sudden, sharp blow or impact.

Act I—Scene 6

Summary

Scene 6 begins with Willy talking to Linda. He continues his conversation with her from Scene 5, describing his loneliness and desperation. At times Willy is overwhelmed with fear that he will not be able to sell anything again. Although Willy is revealing his insecurities to Linda, the Woman who was faintly visible in Scene 5 appears and responds to Willy. The Woman informs Willy that she chose him to be her lover because of his sense of humor. They make plans to meet again next time Willy is in Boston, and then she thanks him for the stockings he brought her.

Commentary

Character Insight

Scene 6 is a pivotal scene because the audience is privy to Willy's guilt over the affair and his subsequent inability to separate memories of Linda from the Woman. It becomes increasingly difficult for Willy to distinguish between the events of the present and the past. Although Willy prefers to believe he is defined by his imagined likability and success as a salesman, in reality, it is the affair that marks his true character. In fact, the affair serves as the defining feature of his being. He is guilt-ridden to the point that he is continually reminded of his infidelity whenever he is in Linda's presence. In addition, the stockings, which he gave to the Woman, serve as a tangible reminder of his transgression. He cannot bear to see Linda mend her stockings because he remembers his infidelity, plus he is forced to acknowledge that he gave Linda's stockings to the Woman. He has betrayed Linda, and he cannot suppress the knowledge.

Act I—Scene 7

Summary

Scene 7 resumes the conversation between Willy and Linda. Linda is unaware of the dialogue exchange from Scene 6, which effectively "interrupted" her discussion with Willy. She repeats her comment from Scene 5 that Willy is an attractive man. Willy, however, is aware of the Woman from Scene 6, and he responds to Linda's comment with a vague apology and a promise to "make it all up to you." Linda is ignorant of what Willy is talking about. Willy observes Linda darning her stockings, and he orders her to throw them away.

Bernard enters, frantically looking for Biff. Willy demands that Bernard give the test answers to Biff. Bernard reveals that he has already been helping Biff cheat, but he cannot help him on the Regents exam. Willy becomes angry at Biff and threatens to beat him. Linda reminds Willy that Biff stole the football, and she also informs him that he is not treating the girls properly. Bernard says Biff is driving without a license. Willy is growing more disturbed with each comment. The Woman from Scene 6 laughs and Willy screams "Shut up!" Bernard continues to criticize Biff until Willy orders him to leave. Linda defends Bernard, but Willy counters her, maintaining that Biff is fine. Linda leaves, and then Willy reverts back to his initial condemnation of Biff at the beginning of the scene.

Commentary

Willy's mental faculties are deteriorating in Scene 7. He is no longer capable of separating the present and the past. In Willy's mind all of the events are occurring at the same time, leaving him confused and bewildered. He does not know if he is in the past or the present, if he still has a chance to make things right with his family, or if he can still achieve success. He remembers the most important events relating to Linda and Biff, but he cannot separate them in his mind. He is in the present at the beginning of the scene, but the sight of Linda's stockings moves him back into the past to the moment of his interlude with the Woman.

Willy's guilt and agitation shift to anger as he focuses on Biff. Willy is already confused, but his anger increases when he learns of Biff's unacceptable behavior. It is not a coincidence that Willy focuses on his own failure—the affair—and on Biff's failure during this scene. Willy denies his own self-incrimination and instead directs all of his castigation upon Biff. Finally, Willy contradicts the majority of the scene when he defends Biff. Rather than admit his son is an imminent failure, Willy ignores the warning signs and praises him instead.

Glossary

liable   subject to the possibility of; likely.

buckle down   to apply oneself energetically; set to work with effort.

worm   an abject, wretched, or contemptible person.

Act I—Scene 8

Summary

Scene 8 shifts back completely to the present. Happy comes downstairs and attempts to walk Willy to bed. Willy tells Happy that he came home because he was having difficulty driving, plus he almost hit someone with the car in Yonkers. Willy recalls his Uncle Ben who became wealthy mining diamonds. Willy regrets not acting on the opportunity to go to Alaska when Ben offered it to him.

Charley comes over and plays cards with Willy. They talk about vitamins, car trouble, and a trip to California. Charley offers Willy a job, but Willy angrily refuses. He reveals his distress over Biff returning to Texas, along with his inability to assist Biff financially. Charley assures him that Biff will be fine. Willy ridicules Charley's inadequacy with tools.

Uncle Ben enters, but he is only visible and audible to Willy. He is not real; he is just another projection of Willy's memory. Willy begins to converse with Ben at the same time he is talking to Charley. As a result, Charley becomes confused when Willy answers questions that Ben is asking. Willy is unable to separate his discussion with Ben from his discussion with Charley, so he becomes flustered and loses his composure. He accuses Charley of cheating. Charley becomes angry and leaves.

Commentary

Willy experiences confusion in Scene 7 as a result of fusing multiple memories. This confusion, along with his anger toward Happy regarding his spending habits, compels him to recall his favorite illusion: Uncle Ben and the diamond mines. Willy cannot accept his recent failures, nor can he accept the fact that his life has been one of mediocrity. Whenever he feels overwhelmed by his lack of success and blasé existence, Willy re-creates his life based on Uncle Ben's lost proposition. If only he had gone to work for Ben, he would be rich. If only he had gone to Alaska, he and the boys would be thriving in the great outdoors.

If only he had had the courage of Ben, he might have established himself as a highly successful salesman.

The fact that Willy observes and speaks to Ben is significant for two reasons. First, he is an interactive creation of Willy's mind. Willy is not just hearing voices; he is actively hallucinating. As far as Willy is concerned, Ben is just as real as Charley. So it is not surprising that Willy becomes confused during the card game. He believes he is talking to two real people who are unaware of each other and engaged in completely different conversations.

Second, Willy refuses to acknowledge that his opportunity to work for Ben no longer exists. Willy talks about Ben's job offer to the boys, and he appears to realize that the opportunity has been lost. However, Willy conjures Ben each time he experiences overwhelming conflict in an attempt to re-create his life by imagining what could have been. Ben's offer still remains valid in Willy's mind because he is incapable of separating the past and the present. Once again, Willy tries to create order by shuffling the past and creating new possibilities.

Glossary

build   to form a sequence according to suit, number, etc.

Ignoramus   an ignorant and stupid person.

Act I—Scene 9

Summary

Scene 9 shifts back to the past. Willy finally meets his brother Ben. Ben is on his way to catch a train, but he and Willy talk briefly about Ben's successful venture into African diamond mining. Willy begs Ben to tell the boys about his father. Willy only remembers vague images of a campfire, a large bearded man, and flute music. Ben describes the large profits their father made selling homemade flutes while traveling across the United States.

Biff and Ben begin boxing. Ben defeats Biff and warns him to use any resources available when fighting a stranger, even if that means being unfair. Linda is uncomfortable as a result of Ben's advice. As Ben prepares to leave, Willy boasts that Brooklyn has all of the qualities of the great outdoors, including animals, large trees, numerous opportunities to hunt, and so forth. He then sends the boys to steal some sand from the apartment construction site. Willy instructs them to remodel the porch in order to demonstrate their building skills.

Charley comes over and warns Willy that the building watchman will have the boys arrested if they are caught again. Willy criticizes Charley and his son Bernard in front of Ben. Bernard arrives, informing everyone that the watchman is pursuing Biff. Willy is momentarily upset, but dismisses his anxiety when Ben compliments Biff's courage.

Charley leaves after Willy insults him again. Willy entreats Ben to stay because he needs someone to talk to. Willy feels insecure and "kind of temporary" since he never had the opportunity to talk to his father. Willy asks Ben to show him how and what to teach the boys. Ben responds by reciting the facts of his African adventure: He was 17 years old when he went in the jungle, 21 years old when he came out, and he was rich.

Commentary

Scene 9 demonstrates Willy's dependence upon his memories and the insecurity that prompts him to rearrange events and facts in an attempt to create order or success.

Once Charley leaves at the end of Scene 8, Willy is free to immerse himself completely in his recollection of Ben's visit. Willy is thrilled by Ben's story of the diamond mines, not only because it proves that individual greatness is possible within the Loman family, but because Willy projects a portion of that success upon himself. Willy believes that he is connected to Ben's accomplishment because Ben offered him a job. It does not matter that Willy refused the position; just the fact that the position was offered links him to Ben and his fortune.

Character Insight

The greatest revelation of Scene 9 comes about with Willy's discussion of his father. Willy is insecure, and he traces his own insecurity to the absence of his father. Having been denied approval from his father, Willy is driven by a need to gain approval and recognition from everyone. This accounts for his "temporary" view of himself. Willy cannot be content with his life, job, or his marriage because he is continually evaluating himself based upon the success of others. As a result, Willy has created a cycle of eager acceptance and rejection of himself. So long as Willy is received favorably, he is momentarily content; however, these moments occur rarely within the play.

More often than not, Willy feels compelled to prove to others that he is successful, as a salesman, as a father, and as an American living in the "great outdoors" of Brooklyn. Willy creates the illusion of success needed to gain approval by rearranging events and facts as he wishes them to be. This reinvention of reality allows him to appear successful to others and to himself, but Willy also realizes that it is only an illusion. Therefore, his satisfaction is fleeting. Whenever Willy acknowledges to himself that he is not successful, in fact is nothing but average, he denies the truth because it is too painful for him to believe that he is a failure. Once again, Willy begins to reconstruct his life in an attempt to create order.

The cycle of acceptance and rejection accounts for Willy's continual contradictions as well. He responds to others, depending on where he is in the cycle. Problems arise because Willy constantly moves back and forth within the cycle; as a result, his comments or behavior must change accordingly. For example, while trying to win approval from

Ben, Willy tells Biff to steal building supplies and remodel the porch. Willy's attitude changes once Bernard announces that the watchman is pursuing Biff. Willy denies that Biff was stealing and denies that he is responsible for Biff's actions. It appears that Willy has failed again because Ben will surely disapprove; however, Ben's praise moves Willy back into eager acceptance of himself and his family.

Glossary

temporary   for a time only; not permanent.

Act I—Scene 10

Summary

Scene 10 shifts back to the present. Linda looks for Willy and finds him talking to himself outside. Willy asks Linda if she still has the diamond watch fob that Ben gave him when he visited. Linda reminds him that he pawned it over 12 years ago to pay for one of Biff's classes. Willy mumbles to himself about Ben and goes for a walk in his slippers.

Biff and Happy come outside and talk with Linda about Willy. Biff is angry and ashamed of Willy's behavior. He asks Linda why she never wrote to him of Willy's condition. Linda becomes upset and reminds Biff that he did not write or provide her with an address where he could be reached. Linda informs Biff that Willy is always excited to hear that Biff is returning home, but he becomes increasingly agitated the closer to Biff's arrival. By the time Biff reaches home, Willy is angry and argumentative.

Linda chastises Biff's tendency to wander from place to place and job to job. She explains that she and Willy are getting older, and that they will die one day. Biff reacts to Linda's statement, but only in relation to her, not Willy. He denies the possibility that she could die anytime soon. She gives Biff an ultimatum: Respect your father or do not come home.

Linda continues to defend Willy, insisting that he is not "crazy" but "exhausted." Linda attributes Willy's behavior to the fact that he is working straight commission, just like a beginning salesman. Willy has been secretly borrowing money from Charley in order to pay the bills. Linda blames Biff and Happy for abandoning their father in order to pursue their own selfish desires.

Biff agrees to stay at home and help out financially, but Linda refuses unless he and Willy can reconcile their differences. Biff reminds her that Willy threw him out of the house because Biff discovered Willy was a fraud. Linda questions Biff, but he refuses to explain his meaning. Linda tells the boys that Willy has attempted to commit suicide several times. She recently discovered a rubber hose attached to the gas pipe. Every day she struggles with the idea of removing it. Biff agrees to stay and find a job, although he does not like the business world. According to Biff, the Lomans should be working outside.

Commentary

Character Insight

Scene 10 belongs to Linda. Up until this point, Linda appears quiet and submissive as she gently encourages Willy and attempts to reconcile her husband and her children. During Scene 10, Linda changes. She is angry, vocal, and determined. In many ways, Linda is the only character who is able to see the truth. She knows that Willy is borrowing money from Charley and lying to her about it. She recognizes that Happy is nothing but an over-achieving womanizer incapable of settling down. She also realizes Biff's drifting is the result of his insecurity and his failure to understand his own needs and desires. Even though Linda "sees" the members of her family as they really are, she is not immune to the denial and contradiction that plagues them. Linda actively participates in the fantasies Willy creates by encouraging his dreams of grandeur. She also chastises the boys when they say or do anything to dispel Willy's imaginings. Thus, even though Linda knows the truth, she actively attempts to conceal it in order to help Willy achieve order in his life. This requires Linda to deny the truth in her outward actions and act in a manner contradictory to the truth. In many ways, Linda's situation is much worse than Willy's: He cannot distinguish between fantasy and reality; she does but acts contrary to it.

Biff's comment that Willy is a "fake" startles Linda, but her reaction is muted so that the audience perceives she is not entirely surprised. Her reaction can even be seen as shock that Biff perceives Willy is not what he appears to be. Even so, Linda gracefully discards Biff's statement and continues with her duty: maintain and protect Willy's fantasy as long as possible. She loves Willy, and that is why she is willing to overlook his irrationality and his cruelty. She will do anything to protect him from reality, from his sons' insensitivity, and ultimately from himself.

Glossary

surly bad-tempered; sullenly rude; hostile and uncivil.

spewing throwing up (something) from or as from the stomach; vomiting.

bastard   a slang term for a person regarded with contempt, hatred, pity, resentment, and so on.

philander   to engage lightly in passing love affairs; make love insincerely.

Act I—Scene 11

Summary

Willy returns from his walk and overhears that some people think he is "crazy," while others just laugh at him. Willy confronts Biff and tells him to go back to Texas. Willy becomes excited when Happy informs him of Biff's plan to speak to Bill Oliver. Biff describes his plan to open his own business. Willy instructs Biff on how much money to ask for, what to wear, how to speak, and what to talk about. First, he directs Biff to be serious and avoid telling jokes, and then he contradicts himself and advises Biff to assume a confident air and tell old stories. Happy recommends going into business with Biff with a line of sporting goods known as the Loman Line.

Throughout the scene, Linda repeatedly says words of encouragement as Biff and Happy describe the plan; however, Willy yells at her for interrupting the conversation. Biff argues with Willy over his treatment of Linda. Linda attempts to stop the argument, but then Willy accuses her of siding with Biff. Willy gives in and goes to bed.

Commentary

For the first time since the play's beginning, everything appears to be coming together for Willy during Scene 11. Although the scene opens with an argument between Willy and Biff, the scene shifts as Biff attempts to reconcile with his father. Up until this point, Willy has relied upon favorite memories—memories in which Biff adores him—rather than accept the disintegrating relationship with his oldest son. Willy feels he has finally achieved a position of authority and respect again. As a result, he immediately begins to dictate what Biff should do when he visits Oliver.

The problem is that Biff wants to be honest with Willy, but Willy will not give him the chance. Each time Biff makes a statement, Willy interrupts him and interprets the partial statement as he wants it to be. Thus, Willy believes Oliver is already funding Biff, while Biff desperately tries to tell him he has not even seen Oliver yet. As the discussion continues,

Biff, Happy, and Linda exaggerate facts, add details, and adopt confident attitudes in order to maintain Willy's fantasy.

Tension arises when Biff and Willy begin to argue over Linda. Even though Linda is determined and vocal within Scene 10, she remains submissive in Willy's presence. Biff resents how Willy treats Linda for two reasons. First, he despises the fact that Willy degrades his mother and insults her, especially when she is merely trying to encourage Willy and the boys. Second, Biff is incapable of forgiving Willy for his affair. As far as Biff is concerned, Willy betrayed his mother, even if the Woman meant "nothing" to him. As a result, Biff assumes a protective air around Linda, and he will defend her against anyone, even his father.

Glossary

exhibitions public shows or displays, as of art, industrial products, athletic feats, and so on.

lick to overcome, vanquish, or control.

Act I—Scene 12

Summary

Linda tells Biff to tell Willy goodnight so that he will end the day on a positive note. Biff borrows money from Happy to buy some new ties. Happy tells Biff to move into his apartment with him. Linda tells Willy the shower needs repair, and he becomes irate. Linda wonders if Bill Oliver will remember Biff, but Willy assures her that he will. Willy proclaims that Biff's experience wandering from job to job will prove valuable. Biff tells Willy and Linda goodnight, and Willy advises Biff to ask for fifteen thousand dollars, and he assures Biff that he (Biff) has "all kinds of greatness" in him. Willy ignores Linda's comments and tells her to quit interrupting. Willy reminisces about one of Biff's football games. Linda asks Willy what Biff knows about his past that he is holding against him, but Willy refuses to answer. Downstairs, Biff finds the rubber tubing behind the heater and removes it.

Commentary

Scene 12 continues the uneasy truce between Willy and Biff. Willy is exhausted, but he seems to be at peace as he anticipates Biff's imminent success. In addition, he feels confident that Howard will give him a job in New York, thereby eliminating the need for travel. He will finally be able to work in town, raise vegetables in the garden, and observe Biff succeed.

Linda's hesitant question suggests that she is not quite convinced that everything is okay. Likewise, Biff does not believe he and Willy have reestablished their relationship. In fact, as he removes the rubber tubing, Biff assumes the peace in the house is only temporary. Linda's uncertainty and Biff's doubt leave the audience with the expectation that the "order" achieved is only short-lived.

Glossary

buck up [Informal]to cheer up.

caliber degree of worth or value of a person or thing; quality or ability.

Hercules in Greek and Roman myth, the son of Zeus and Alcmene, renowned for his strength and courage, especially, as shown in his performance of twelve labors imposed on him.

Act II—Scene 1

Summary

Act II begins the next morning. Biff and Happy have already gone, and Linda serves Willy breakfast. Biff has gone to borrow money from Bill Oliver so he can open the sporting goods line. Willy is excited and confident that Biff will obtain the money and finally be successful. Willy dreams of growing vegetables, moving to the country, and building two guest houses for the boys and their wives. Willy is convinced that everything is getting better, and he feels certain Howard will give him a job in New York.

Linda reminds Willy to request an advance because there is not enough money to pay the bills. Willy's mood changes, and he becomes angry. He complains about the Studebaker, as well as the refrigerator. Linda points out that the mortgage will be paid in full after this month. Willy reminisces about the house and the work he put into it during the last 25 years. Willy is supposed to meet Biff and Happy at Frank's Chop House for a surprise dinner. He instructs Linda again to quit repairing her stockings. Biff calls Linda, and she tells him Willy removed the rubber pipe, but Biff informs her that he got rid of the pipe himself.

Commentary

A shift takes place between Act I and Act II. This first scene seems very promising because things appear to be working out. Although Act I, Scene 12 ends amicably, the only reason Biff and Willy are no longer fighting is because it is bedtime. If the scene continued, another argument would likely erupt. Surprisingly enough, things still remain peaceful in the morning, when Act II begins. Biff is finally pursuing gainful employment, and Willy is more optimistic and confident than he has been throughout the entire play. He does not exaggerate anything, nor is he afflicted by distant memories of happier times. He is cordial to Linda, and resolute in his decision to confront Howard. Linda is relieved and ecstatic that Willy is acting like his old self. It appears that everything is finally looking up for Willy and his family.

In reality, nothing has changed. Willy's rapid mood change when Linda mentions the bills demonstrates his inability to achieve order in his life. He feels he is racing the clock when it comes to material items such as the car, the refrigerator, and even the house. Willy fails to recognize that the very things he complains about provide business to a salesman. For example, once he pays off the refrigerator it begins to need service. Sooner or later, he will be forced to purchase another one. As a salesman, he depends upon customer needs and desires, yet he does not see the connection between supply and demand in relation to himself. Ironically, he holds out from doing what he tries to convince his clients to do: buy more products.

The eruption in Willy's calm demeanor leads to a series of contradictions in the scene. He marvels over the house and the joyful memories of working on it. Linda assumes her previous role of assuring and encouraging him in order to restore Willy to his previous serenity. If he makes a statement, such as what an accomplishment it is to pay off a mortgage or how well the house is built, she agrees with him. However, the contradiction comes when Willy negates his own sense of satisfaction by remarking that it is all for nothing. Once again, Willy is caught in a cycle of acceptance and rejection, even of himself. He congratulates himself for working many years to pay off the house, but then he deflates himself and considers all of his work pointless.

Linda realizes that Willy is caught in the cycle again, but she is still optimistic because she believes he has given up his thoughts of suicide. She considers his attitude over the bills and the house as nothing serious, because (she believes) he removed the rubber hose. At least now she does not have to worry about Willy asphyxiating himself with gas from the heater.

Style & Language

Linda is also living in denial. Even when Biff tells her that he removed the hose, she remains hopeful that everything will be okay. However, her doubt and fear are revealed by her desperation as she describes Willy as "a little boat looking for a harbor," and as she pleads with Biff to "save his life." She realizes that suicide is still a possibility, but she refuses to acknowledge it.

Glossary

saccharine   a sugar substitute in diabetic diets.

Act II—Scene 2

Summary

Willy goes to the office with the intention of asking Howard for a New York position. Howard tells Willy about his new recorder and demonstrates how it works. Howard plays recordings of his children and his wife and convinces Willy to buy a recorder. Willy expresses his desire to work in New York rather than continue traveling. Howard hesitates until Willy reminds him of the Christmas party and Howard's promise to give Willy an in-town job if possible. Howard says there are no openings at the moment. Willy begs Howard for a job, each time asking for less money, but Howard insists that a job is not available.

In an effort to convince Howard, Willy resorts to old memories of his glory days when he worked for Howard's father. In addition, Willy attempts to explain why he became a salesman. He describes Dave Singleman, a well-respected professional salesman who made a lasting impression on people and was publicly mourned when he died. Howard remains impassive to Willy's entreaties and instead informs Willy that Willy can no longer work for the company. Howard advises Willy to appeal to Biff and Happy for financial assistance, and he instructs Willy to return his sample cases by the end of the week.

Commentary

Willy's world begins crashing down around him during Scene 2. Willy does not like to deal with Howard because his boss fails to appreciate him; however, Willy is confident that Howard will accept his request to work in New York. Willy's confidence is the result of Linda's encouragement during Scene 1 and Biff's appointment with Oliver. Just as Willy projected Ben's success onto himself during Act I, Scene 9, so he envisions his own victory with Howard because of Biff's imminent success with Oliver.

Character Insight

Howard is a bottom-line businessman who sees Willy as a tired old salesman relying on his ability to talk rather than his ability to sell. Howard sympathizes with Willy, but he is not willing to give him a job in New York for two reasons. First, a New York job would give

Willy a base salary again. Howard is aware that Willy's sales have not been adequate for some time; it was for this reason that he withdrew Willy's salary and put him on commission. By keeping Willy on commission, Howard is only obligated to pay Willy according to his gross sales. If Willy does not sell well, it does not adversely affect the company. Second, Howard does not want Willy in New York because he would have to deal with him every day. Howard does not dislike Willy, but he tires of Willy's rambling exaggerations and references to times when Willy worked for Howard's father. Having Willy in New York would be a nuisance.

It is important to note that Howard does not fire Willy out of spite. It is a business decision that Howard has been putting off for some time. Willy's behavior during the interview prompts Howard to act upon his decision. At first Howard is sympathetic to Willy's desire to work in New York, but he does not want him there, and so he emphasizes the fact that Willy is a "road man." At this point, Howard still intends to keep Willy, in spite of his inconsistent behavior in the past.

Willy realizes that he is not getting through to Howard, so he resorts to his safety mechanism: When the present is not tolerable, revert to the past. Willy attempts to persuade Howard by reminding him that he named him as a child. Once this fails, Willy is forced to move deeper into the past. He rationalizes that Howard will change his mind if he will only listen to Willy's story of Dave Singleman. Willy describes Singleman's success and admiration so vividly because he believes he can claim some of Singleman's success for himself. If he projects these traits to Howard, then Howard cannot refuse him. Although Howard does not change his mind, he listens to Willy considerately. Nevertheless, Willy's exaggeration makes Howard impatient and finally compels him to fire Willy.

Howard tells Willy to look to his family for support. Even at the end of the scene, Howard should not be judged too harshly. His motto is "business is business," and therefore business must go on. He realizes that Willy is no longer just an ineffective salesman; now his behavior makes him an embarrassment to the company and a source of potential loss of customers and revenue. Willy's attempt to create order—by working in New York and by using his memories to obtain the New York job—has effectively backfired, leaving him without a job, without financial security, and without his identity as a "salesman."

Glossary

self-reliance reliance on one's own judgment, abilities, etc.

cut and dried an expression meaning "strictly business" without time for or need of pleasantries.

Act II–Scene 3

Summary

Howard's office disappears as Scene 3 shifts into the past. Ben approaches Willy on his way to Alaska. Willy asks Ben for advice because things are not going as planned. Ben offers Willy a job overseeing his timberland in Alaska, and Willy accepts. Linda comes back and scolds Ben for putting ideas of Alaska in Willy's head. She reminds Willy of his promising future as a salesman, as well as the successful Dave Singleman. Willy attempts to convince Ben that his job as a salesman is just as remarkable as working in Alaska. Willy is convinced he and the boys will become just as rich and successful as Ben, even though they remain in Brooklyn.

Commentary

The placement of Scene 3 makes it particularly effective. Willy attempts to deal with what has happened with Howard and escape from it at the same time by reverting back to Ben. Ben has always been successful, so he is the natural choice for advice. Willy wants Ben to analyze the current situation and tell him what to do. Instead, Ben offers Willy a job in Alaska—the same offer he made when he actually visited in the past—but Willy can no longer separate the past from the present; they are blending together.

Character Insight

The fact that Willy turns down the offer is very poignant in light of what happened in Scene 2. In the past, Willy refused Ben's offer because he was determined to be a successful salesman, just like Dave Singleman. Now that he has been fired, he is overwhelmed by his feelings: regret, for not accepting Ben's offer and moving to Alaska; shame, for losing his job; and despair, for having devoted his life to a company that could discard him so easily.

Act II—Scene 4

Summary

Scene 4 continues in the past. Willy, Linda, and Happy are preparing to go to Ebbet's Field, to watch Biff play football. Willy frantically searches for the pennants while Happy and Bernard argue over who will carry Biff's football helmet. Biff plans to score a touchdown for Willy. Charley comes over, pretending he is unaware that today is Biff's game. Charley's behavior infuriates Willy.

Commentary

Willy is free falling into his memories of the past. He is moving directly from one memory to the next in a desperate attempt to deny the present and create order from his disordered life. He has been unhappy with his lack of success, but he could cope with that by exaggerating his sales and focusing on better times. Now having lost his job, he is in a difficult situation because he will be forced to admit failure to Linda and the boys. This prompts the memory merry-go-round that Willy is on during Scenes 3 and 4. First he goes to Ben for solace, but that does not work. He is forced to acknowledge that he gave up his one opportunity for great success.

Rather than dwell on the idea that he is a failure, Willy then goes back to his favorite memories of Biff. As his son prepares for the Ebbet's Field game, Biff symbolizes the greatness Willy still believes is possible to achieve. Imminent greatness, along with the fact that Biff respects him as a loving father and authority figure, works to create an ideal fantasy. Willy has found the order he desires, and he can keep it if he just remains in this moment in time.

Act II—Scene 5

Summary

Scene 5 shifts back to the present. Willy goes to Charley's office where the secretary, Jenny, overhears him talking to himself. Willy is still enjoying his reverie from Scene 4. Willy is taunting someone about Biff's impending football game and the touchdown he has promised to make for Willy. Willy's daydream ends when he sees Bernard. Willy discovers that Bernard is very successful and that he will soon be staying with rich friends who have their own tennis courts. Willy tells Bernard that Biff is closing a business venture with Bill Oliver. Willy also states that Oliver recruited Biff and is paying his expenses.

Willy asks Bernard how he managed to succeed so well, while Biff did so poorly. According to Willy, Biff's life took a turn for the worse after the Ebbet's Field game. Bernard reminds Willy that Biff failed math, and as a result, he did not graduate. Bernard questions why Biff did not attend summer school. Willy is not sure why he did not go.

Bernard remembers that Biff traveled to Boston to visit Willy and talk about his future. He then tells Willy that Biff burned his home-made University of Virginia tennis shoes and got into a fistfight with him when he returned. Bernard asks Willy what happened to Biff in Boston. At this point, Willy becomes angry and resentful.

Commentary

Scene 5 builds upon the desperation established in Scene 2. Willy has been borrowing money from Charley for weeks in order to pay the bills. Since he has always been jealous of Charley, this is extremely difficult for him to do. However, Charley gives Willy what he needs and does his best not to humiliate him. In many ways, Charley is a much better friend to Willy than anyone else is, even though Willy denies this to himself.

Willy is "genuinely shocked, pained, and happy" to learn of Bernard's achievements. It is difficult for him to talk with Bernard because Bernard has done so well, while Biff has not. Willy cannot help but compare the two men now, since he continually compared them as children. Although Willy is happy for Bernard and certainly does not wish him any ill, it is not easy for him to observe Bernard's success. Willy had always predicted that Biff would surpass the "anemic" Bernard, due to strength and the fact that he was "well-liked." This is yet another example of the failure of Willy's predictions. Not only is Bernard more prosperous than Biff, but Willy is forced to borrow money from Bernard's father, a man that he has always envied.

It is important to note that Willy uses the past to attempt to create order in a present that is no longer bearable. However, Willy selectively chooses and arranges his memories and facts in a way that is pleasing to him. He does not randomly choose memories, nor does he allow himself to remember everything. Instead he tries to carefully edit out anything that could disrupt the order he desires. The conversation between Bernard and Willy is unsettling to Willy because it awakens unbidden memories that he prefers to deny.

Theme

Up until this point, Willy blames Biff's failures on laziness and lack of motivation, but after Howard fires him, Willy begins to consider that perhaps he is responsible in some way: "It keeps going around in my mind, maybe I did something to him. I got nothing to give him." Willy has muddled this idea around but has not thought of what he might have done wrong. Bernard suggests that something else is behind Biff's downward spiral since high school, and he hints that Willy is connected to the change in Biff. Once Bernard connects the change in Biff to Biff's Boston visit, Willy knows what he did wrong. He becomes defensive toward Bernard as a way of denying his own culpability. He refuses to admit anything to Bernard, but Willy suspects that he has not only ruined his own life, but his son's as well.

Act II—Scene 6

Summary

Charley comes in the office as Bernard leaves. Charley tells Willy that Bernard will present a case before the Supreme Court. Charley gives Willy $50, but Willy asks for more because of his insurance payment. Charley offers Willy a job, but Willy refuses repeatedly. Charley is offended and becomes angry; however, he gives Willy the money. Willy reveals that Howard fired him. Once again Charley attempts to convince Willy to work for him, but Willy refuses and will not explain why. Willy remarks that an individual is "worth more dead than alive."

Commentary

Scene 6 represents Willy's last chance to put his life back together. Although Charley freely gives Willy the money that he needs, he offers Willy the opportunity to start his life over and end the charade he is living. In many ways, Charley's proposition can be paralleled to Ben's. Both men present Willy with a job that guarantees a measure of success, along with attractive benefits. Ben gave him the chance to work outdoors and possibly become rich, while Charley gives him the chance to earn a reasonable income without traveling.

Character Insight

Pride causes Willy to lose both of his chances. He turned down Ben's job because he wanted to prove to his brother that he could do just as well in Brooklyn. He turns Charley down because he has always been jealous of the fact that Charley owns his own business. In the past, Willy ridiculed Charley, just as he used to ridicule Bernard, so he feels that working for Charley now would be a humiliation. It is perfectly fine with Willy to borrow money from Charley secretly, but he does not want to be associated with Charley as an employer.

Charley confronts Willy with the truth about his job: Willy is a salesman, and a salesman is defined by what he can sell. Anything that cannot be sold is irrelevant and of no value. If the salesman cannot sell anything, then he is worthless. The fact that Charley can adequately describe Willy's job, as well as Willy's character, along with the fact that he genuinely wants to help him, forces Willy to acknowledge that Charley is his "only friend."

Act II—Scene 7

Summary

Scene 7 takes place in a local restaurant. Happy chats with Stanley, the waiter, and Stanley is impressed because Happy can predict when beautiful women will enter the café. Happy flirts with Miss Forsythe, a young woman seated at the next table. Biff enters, and Happy informs him that the girl is on duty. Happy instructs her to cancel her appointment and find a friend. Biff is upset. He went to Oliver's office and waited six hours to see him, but Oliver did not remember him at all. Biff was just a shipping clerk when he worked for Oliver, not a salesman. Biff stole Oliver's fountain pen. Happy directs Biff not to reveal to Willy what happened.

Commentary

Character Insight

Scene 7 provides the audience with insight into Happy's character. Happy is defined by his sexuality and desire for power. He wants everyone to believe he is an assistant buyer when he is really the "assistant to the assistant." Happy uses his good looks and sexual prowess as a means of gaining power over others, both females and males. For example, he does not care anything for Miss Forsythe, and it is later revealed that she is a prostitute, but he tells her to cancel her date and find someone to bring along with her. Happy enjoys commanding women. Here he gives Miss Forsythe an order simply because he knows she will do it. This gives him satisfaction and pleasure. Later, he will gain sexual pleasure from her or her friend.

Happy also relishes the fact that "respectable" women cannot resist him. He has seduced the fiancées of three executives just to gain pleasure and power. He thrives on sexual gratification, but even more than that, Happy savors the knowledge that he has ruined women engaged to men he works for and also despises. He states, "I hate myself for it. Because I don't want the girl, and, still, I take it and—I love it!" Happy is similar to Willy in two ways. Both deny their positions and exaggerate details in order to aggrandize themselves, and sexual interludes are the defining moments of both of their lives. Willy's life revolves around his attempt to forget his affair with the Woman, while Happy's life revolves around an active pursuit of affairs with many women.

Glossary

strudel   a kind of pastry; here the term refers to a prostitute.

Act II—Scene 8

Summary

Willy joins Happy and Biff in the restaurant. Biff says he wants to have a discussion based on facts only. Biff does not know who originally said he was a salesman for Bill Oliver, when he was actually just a shipping clerk. Willy tells the boys that Howard fired him. Biff tries to explain what happened at Oliver's office, but Willy keeps interrupting him. Biff and Willy argue, and Willy accuses Biff of offending Oliver. Biff is exasperated.

Commentary

Scene 8 is significant because it is begins to build the tension that erupts in Scene 9, ultimately leading to the final confrontation between Willy and Biff in Scene 13.

Character Insight

For the first time in his life, Biff attempts to address his life as it really is. Waiting for Oliver makes Biff realize he has been living a lie. All this time, Biff has directed his anger and resentment toward Willy because he considers him a "fake." However, Biff is his father's son, just like Happy. He too creates a favorable past for himself—or an unhappy childhood—in order to justify the course his life has taken. As a result, Scene 8 is a turning point for Biff. He consciously chooses reality over fantasy. He would rather deal with the facts, as strange and disturbing as they may be, than reinvent events to suit his purpose.

Scene 8 is important for Willy because he is also truthful about his situation. For once he does not attempt to sugarcoat his job or his success for the boys. However, Willy contradicts his own willingness to accept reality as he continues to force Biff into a lie. Willy cannot allow Biff to fail because that will only magnify his own breakdown. He constantly interrupts Biff while he is talking for two reasons: to prevent Biff from telling the truth and to interpret the events as he wants them to be. Happy contributes to Willy's fantasy by contradicting Biff each time Biff tries to be honest. So as Biff makes an effort to finally achieve order by admitting the truth, Willy and Happy likewise attempt to create order by concealing the truth.

Act II–Scene 9

Summary

Scene 9 continues primarily in the restaurant, although the house is lit when Linda appears. Willy is still sitting at the table with Biff and Happy. Biff attempts to describe his visit to Oliver, but Willy does not hear him. Instead he hears young Bernard inform Linda that Biff failed math and will not graduate. Bernard also tells her that Biff took a train to Boston to talk with Willy. The exchange between Linda and Bernard ends as Biff finishes explaining why he took Oliver's pen; however, Willy did not hear Biff's explanation.

Willy overhears the operator at a hotel ring his room. Willy answers the operator, telling her he is not available. Biff is confused and upset because Willy is behaving irrationally. Willy tells Biff that he is "no good for anything," until Biff states that he is supposed to meet with Oliver and his partner about the Florida idea. This brings Willy back to the present. Willy becomes angry because Biff refuses to meet with Oliver and his partner since he stole the fountain pen. Biff then admits that he does not have an appointment with Oliver after all, that he only went to Oliver because of Willy.

Willy slips back into the past. The Woman from Act I, Scene 6 asks if he plans to open the door. Willy stumbles off in the restaurant, looking for a door. Biff begs Happy to help Willy, and he shows Happy the rubber hose he found. Happy refuses and blames Biff for Willy's condition. Happy tells the girls that Willy is not his father and then leaves with the girls without paying the tab.

Commentary

Willy is mentally collapsing at this point. He had difficulty distinguishing between the past and present earlier in the play, but the possibility of things getting better still existed. By Scene 9, Willy knows that all is lost—both his job and Biff's chance of success—so he resorts to the past to escape the present. Biff's failure with Oliver immediately moves Willy back to his son's failure in high school. As Biff tries to explain what happened with Oliver, Willy is caught in the past, still trying to understand what it is that caused Biff to "lay down" in high school and how that connects to his failure today. Willy is desperately trying to regain order in the present by making sense of the past.

Learning that Biff stole Oliver's pen temporarily brings Willy out of the past. Willy feels responsible for Biff's actions, and he immediately moves back into the past to find justification for the theft. Biff states, "I didn't exactly steal it [the pen]!" but it is impossible for Willy or the audience to believe this based on his previous record that includes stealing the football, as well as the building materials. Willy is partially to blame for Biff's actions simply because he sanctioned his behavior every time before by not making Biff face the consequences. Therefore, because Willy taught Biff that he did not have to follow rules in high school, his behavior in the present is a reflection of his previous conditioning. As a result, Willy bears the primary responsibility for Biff's present failure.

Willy loses his grip on reality as the the scene progresses and blends Young Bernard, the hotel operator, and the Woman into his conversation with Biff. Once Biff realizes his father is hallucinating, he is compelled to lie to Willy in order to restore him to his senses. The only way he can effectively regain order for Willy is to deny his own need to accept reality. As a result, Biff is forced to contradict his own principles rather than watch his father fall apart before his eyes.

Act II—Scene 10

Summary

Scene 10 begins in a hotel room. The Woman tells Willy that he has "ruined" her and that she will send him in to the buyers immediately whenever he is in Boston. They are in the process of getting dressed when someone knocks on the door. Willy orders the Woman to remain in the bathroom. Biff comes in and tells Willy that he failed math and will not graduate. Willy decides to leave immediately so that he can talk with Biff's teacher before the school closes for the summer. The Woman comes out of the bathroom. Willy pretends that she is simply borrowing his bathroom, and he tells her to leave, but she refuses until he gives her the stockings he promised. Willy orders Biff to help him pack, but Biff resists. Biff calls Willy a liar and a "phony little fake." The scene shifts back to the restaurant. Stanley helps Willy to the door because he is disoriented. Stanley gives him directions to a feed store.

Commentary

Theme

Scene 10 is the key to the play. Willy is finally forced to confront the point of disorder in his life. It is true that Willy has always exaggerated events and details to become "well-liked"; however, up until the affair, Willy had not sacrificed his principles or betrayed his family. Willy blames his behavior on loneliness, but it is the result of his need for attention. The affair is a betrayal of Linda and the boys, who center their lives on him. Once he cheats on Linda, Willy denigrates himself, and this diminution of his character is unrecoverable.

A selective process governs Willy's habit of denying the present in favor of a more satisfactory past. Willy does not randomly choose memories, nor does he allow himself to remember everything. For example, during Scene 5, Willy becomes defensive when questioned by Bernard. He reacts in this manner because Bernard triggers memories of the affair. Willy knows he was unfaithful to Linda, but he has successfully pushed that memory to the back of his mind because of the guilt associated with it. Bernard's question brings the affair to the front of Willy's mind, and he can no longer selectively forget it.

During Scene 9, Willy desperately sorts through memories of Biff's childhood in order to explain to himself why Biff failed with Oliver. He cannot understand why Biff let his last opportunity for success pass him by. It is only when Biff reveals his reason for going to see Oliver that Willy finally understands: "Why did I go? Why did I go? Look at you! Look at what's become of you!" Biff went to see Oliver to please his father and to prevent Willy from suffering a complete mental breakdown. Biff fails with Oliver, just as he did in high school, and Willy is to blame for failures of both the past and present. Even though Biff still wants to satisfy Willy, he cannot because his esteem for his father has been irreparably damaged by knowledge of the affair.

During Scene 10, once Biff discovers that his father is not perfect, and even worse, that he is a traitor to his mother, Biff loses all respect for Willy. He realizes that everything Willy said to him means nothing. The affair negates all of Willy's tales of greatness that have motivated Biff up to this point. Why should he attend summer school or hold a steady job? Need for his father's approval no longer guides his actions. As a result, Willy is responsible for Biff's downward spiral. Biff did not attend summer school or graduate because of Willy's perfidy. Now he is incapable of achieving success because he possesses no faith in his father or himself.

Glossary

self-centered   occupied or concerned only with one's own affairs; egocentric; selfish.

ruin   to deprive (a woman) of chastity.

chippie   [Slang] a promiscuous young woman or a prostitute.

Act II—Scene 11

Summary

Scene 11 takes place at home. Linda is furious with the boys because they left Willy at the restaurant. She orders them out of the house. Happy attempts to give her flowers, but she knocks them to the floor and then orders him to clean it up. Biff insists on talking with Willy, but Linda forbids him. Willy is outside planting his garden.

Commentary

Scene 11 parallels Act I, Scene 10. Linda is no longer submissive and cowed. Willy intimidates and criticizes her into silence throughout much of the play; however, when Willy is absent, Linda becomes outspoken, especially when defending Willy to their sons. At this point, Linda also realizes that all is lost. Willy is defeated not only because he has lost his job, but also because there is no possibility of reconciliation with Biff. Linda knows that any interaction between Willy and Biff from this point on will only lead to confrontation, and this may ultimately lead to Willy's demise. As a result, she is harsh to Biff for several reasons. First, she is acting defensively to prevent further harm to Willy. Second, she feels betrayed by her own sons who promised to help her "save" Willy. Third, she is disturbed to see Willy's mental faculties so deteriorated that he attempts to plant a garden in the middle of the night. Last, she is desperate because she knows Willy's mental condition will not recover from this. All is lost.

Glossary

louse   [Slang] a person regarded as mean, contemptible, etc.

babble   to make incoherent sounds, as a baby does; to prattle or talk too much or foolishly.

Act II—Scene 12

Summary

Scene 12 begins in the backyard. Willy is measuring the dimensions of the garden and talking to himself. Ben enters and discusses Willy's plan to commit suicide. Ben cautions Willy that the insurance company might refuse to pay the life insurance policy. Willy imagines Biff's reaction to a grand funeral. Willy wants Biff to realize that his father was "known" and respected throughout New England. Ben warns him that Biff will consider him a coward.

Commentary

Willy openly discusses his plan to commit suicide in Scene 12. It is only natural that he confers with Ben because Ben will not reveal Willy's intentions, and he represents success. This is Willy's last opportunity to earn a substantial amount of money and acquire the respect of his older brother. In addition, Willy wants to make amends to Linda for betraying her. Leaving her financially stable will help alleviate the guilt that he bears, even though he still cannot admit his unfaithfulness. As a result, suicide serves as a means for Willy to deny his past, establish order and financial stability for his wife, and gain the respect of his idol.

Willy's only hesitation is his uncertainty regarding Biff. Ben warns Willy that Biff will resent him, but Willy wants to believe, and therefore chooses to believe, that Biff will respect him for sacrificing his life. He is certain that Biff will finally forgive him for being unfaithful to Linda. However, Willy does not stop to consider that Biff resents him not only for the affair, but also for his dishonesty. Ben points out that Biff would see committing suicide in order to collect a life insurance policy as just another form of dishonesty. Willy fails to acknowledge this and refuses to believe that Biff could react negatively to his suicide.

Willy's plan to commit suicide is ironic because Willy has been governed by his need for acceptance from an absent father. His plan will absent him from his own son and cause Biff to hate him.

Glossary

thunderstruck   struck with amazement.

ruddiness   a red or reddish color or complexion.

Act II—Scene 13

Summary

Biff informs Willy that he is leaving home forever, severing all ties with the family. Willy refuses to shake Biff's hand and tells him to "rot in hell if you leave this house!" Willy accuses Biff of wasting his life out of spite. Biff confronts Willy with the rubber hose and tells him he will not pity him if he commits suicide. Biff blames Willy for his inability to keep a steady job. According to Biff, the Lomans have not ever been truthful with one another or themselves. Biff is tired of fighting and blaming Willy for his own lack of success. Biff says that he and Willy are nothing but ordinary people who could easily be replaced by others. He and his father argue, and, when Biff breaks down and cries, holding onto Willy, Willy is amazed and "elevated" at Biff's love for him.

Commentary

Character Insight

Scene 13 provides the final break between Willy and Biff. Both men struggle with their emotions and their inability to reconcile. Biff realizes in Scene 8 that he has been reinventing facts just like Willy. His realization is significant because once he verbalizes it to Willy, Linda, and Happy during Scene 13 he separates himself from them. Biff refuses to participate in the charade any longer. He chooses to accept himself on his own terms, not the way Willy imagines or desires him to be. His choice alienates him from Linda and Happy who are committed to maintaining Willy's fantasies at all costs. Biff is able to see beyond their shortsightedness because he realizes that denying reality is more dangerous and costly in the long run. This is exactly the trap Willy is caught in.

For Willy to admit that he is "a dime a dozen" is too painful. Such an admission would force him to openly contradict every grand story he has ever told or is planning to tell. Willy cannot deprive himself of his dreams by admitting he is only average. Even though he knows that he has failed his family, he cannot acknowledge such failure openly; instead, only Ben can share in this revelation. As a result, it is not surprising that Willy responds so dramatically to Biff's claim that their lives have been based on deception. To condemn Willy's fantasies is to threaten Willy's existence. Biff levels the final blow when he confronts Willy with the rubber hose. Not only does Biff force Willy to recognize the hose and his suicidal intention, but in so doing, Biff destroys Willy's dream that his suicide will redeem him.

Glossary

spite   a mean or evil feeling toward another, characterized by the inclination to hurt, humiliate, annoy, frustrate, and so on; ill will; malice.

blow   [Informal] to brag; boast.

contemptuous   full of contempt; scornful or disdainful.

dime a dozen   an expression used to imply that something is available in large quantities. The fact that the item is not rare suggests that it is not of great value.

mutt   a mixed-breed dog; an insult if applied to an individual.

Act II—Scene 14

Summary

Willy is overwhelmed by Biff's reaction at the end of Scene 13. He is amazed that Biff cares for him. Everyone goes to bed, but Willy lingers because Ben has reappeared. Ben reminds him of the $20,000 insurance policy. Willy is convinced that Biff will respect him even more if he commits suicide in order to gain the policy. Willy drives away.

Linda, Biff, Happy, Charley, and Bernard gather together at Willy's grave.

Commentary

Willy finally achieves a sense of peace and order in Scene 14 because he knows Biff loves him. He is overwhelmed by the fact that his estranged son wept for him. For the first time in the play, Willy has received the attention and respect that he desires. But, even though Biff cries to his father because he can no longer pretend, Willy still tries to manipulate reality. Biff's reaction gives Willy the order he has been seeking, but it also compels him to create an even more desirable future. Willy believes he has been given another opportunity to achieve success now that he is reconciled to Biff. He can make Biff love him even more by taking charge of the future and leaving him the insurance money.

Literary Device

It is symbolic that Ben convinces Willy to commit suicide. Ben transforms suicide into a final, brief opportunity that must be seized. In the immediacy of the situation, fearing he will lose this chance and fail yet again, Willy denies his own son's statement, "There'll be no pity for you, you hear it? No pity!"

Requiem

Summary

The requiem takes place at Willy's grave. Linda does not understand why none of the people Willy knew bothered to come to the funeral. Happy is angry that Willy committed suicide, while Biff says that Willy "didn't know who he was." Charley tells them that a salesman's life depends upon dreams. Happy is determined to fulfill Willy's dreams, but Biff plans to leave Brooklyn. Linda tells Willy that she keeps waiting for him to come home. She does not understand why he killed himself because of money. According to Linda, they are finally debt-free.

Commentary

Style & Language

It is important to note that Miller begins and ends the play with Linda. The nervous anxiety that Linda feels when calling out for Willy in Act I, Scene 1 parallels the disquieting grief demonstrated at the end when she calls out to him again.

Willy has contradicted his own intentions. Rather than illustrate the fact that he was "well-liked," his unimpressive funeral demonstrates his mediocrity. It is significant that Charley defends Willy's suicide since Willy always felt jealous and threatened by Charley. Charley is Willy's only true friend in the play, and he recognizes Willy's need for acknowledgment and appreciation. Just as he bailed Willy out when he needed money, so Charley bails him out when no one else understands his suicide.

Theme

Willy's suicide cannot be justified because it defies his own intentions. Willy believes his suicide will resolve the disorder in his life by assuaging any pain he caused Linda, winning Biff's respect, and demonstrating his popularity as a salesman and individual. In reality, he denies Linda a debt-free husband, Biff a reconciled father, and Happy an improved role model. Thus Willy's refusal to accept life on its own terms results in nothing but disorder and fragmentation for those he loves most.

Glossary

requiem a Mass for one or more deceased persons; any musical service, hymn, or dirge for the dead.

CHARACTER ANALYSES

The following critical analyses delve into the physical, emotional, and psychological traits of the literary work's major characters so that you might better understand what motivates these characters. The writer of this study guide provides this scholarship as an educational tool by which you may compare your own interpretations of the characters. Before reading the character analyses that follow, consider first writing your own short essays on the characters as an exercise by which you can test your understanding of the original literary work. Then, compare your essays to those that follow, noting discrepancies between the two. If your essays appear lacking, that might indicate that you need to re-read the original literary work or re-familiarize yourself with the major characters.

Willy Loman

Death of a Salesman is Willy's play. Everything revolves around his actions during the last 24 hours of his life. All of the characters act in response to Willy, whether in the present or in Willy's recollection of the past. Willy's character, emotions, motivations, and destiny are developed through his interactions with others. The problem arises, however, because Willy reacts to characters in the present, while simultaneously responding to different characters and different situations in the past. The result is Willy's trademark behavior: contradictory, somewhat angry, and often obsessive.

Willy is an individual who craves attention and is governed by a desire for success. He constantly refers to his older brother Ben, who made a fortune in diamond mining in Africa, because he represents all the things Willy desires for himself and his sons. Willy is forced to work for Howard, the son of his old boss, who fails to appreciate Willy's previous sales experience and expertise. Ben, on the other hand, simply abandoned the city, explored the American and African continents, and went to work for himself. As a result, after four years in the jungle, Ben was a rich man at the age of 21, while Willy must struggle to convince Howard to let him work in New York for a reduced salary after working for the company for 34 years. Willy does not envy Ben, but looks to him as model of success.

The play begins and ends in the present, and the plot occurs during the last two days of Willy's life; however, a large portion of the play consists of Willy's fragmented memories, recollections, and re-creations of the past, which are spliced in between scenes taking place in the present. Willy not only remembers an event but also relives it, engaging himself in the situation as if it is happening for the first time. As the play progresses, Willy becomes more irrational and is not able to transition between his memory of the past and the reality of the present.

Willy's memories are key to understanding his character. He carefully selects memories or re-creates past events in order to devise situations in which he is successful or to justify his current lack of prosperity. For example, Willy recalls Ben and the job he offered to Willy after being fired by Howard. Willy is unable to cope with the idea that he has failed, so he relives Ben's visit. The memory allows Willy to deny the truth and its consequences—facing Linda and the boys after being fired—and to establish temporary order in his disrupted life. At other times, Willy proudly recalls memories of Biff's last football game because it is more pleasant to re-create the past in which Biff adored him and wanted to score a touchdown in his name, rather than face the present where he is at odds with his own son.

Willy's constant movement from the present to the past results in his contradictory nature. Although he fondly remembers Biff as a teenager, he is unable to communicate with Biff in the present. As a result, he praises Biff in one breath, while criticizing him in the next. The cause of Willy's inconsistent behavior is his unbidden memories of a long-ago affair, which he forgets or chooses not to remember until the end of Act II. It is difficult enough for Willy to deal with Howard, his buyers (or lack of buyers), and the everyday reminders that he is not a great salesman like Dave Singleman; however, it is even more insufferable for Willy to accept the idea that he is a failure in his son's eyes.

Prior to the Boston trip, Biff, more than anyone, sincerely believes in Willy's success, potential, and inevitable greatness. Willy is able to achieve the success and notoriety he desires only through Biff, but this changes when Biff learns of the affair. After the Boston trip, Willy tries to regain the success he once had by focusing on memories or events prior to the discovery of the affair. It is not surprising that Willy contradicts himself when speaking in the present about Biff or to him, for although Willy chooses to remember Biff as he used to be, he cannot eradicate the words Biff spoke to him in Boston: "You fake! You phony little fake!"

Willy perceives himself as a failure: He is not Dave Singleman. He is just a mediocre salesman who has only made monumental sales in his imagination. Now that he is growing old and less productive, the company he helped to build fires him. He regrets being unfaithful to his wife, even though he will never admit the affair to her. He is no longer a respectable man in Biff's eyes. Biff recognizes Willy's tendency to exaggerate or reconstruct reality and is no longer a willing participant in Willy's fantasy. By the end of the play, Willy is overwhelmed; he can no longer deny his failures when they become too many to deal with. Instead, he seeks a solution in suicide. Willy reasons he can finally be a success because his life insurance policy will in some way compensate Linda for his affair. Additionally, Biff will consider him a martyr and respect him after witnessing the large funeral and many mourners Willy is sure will attend.

Biff Loman

Biff is a catalyst. He drives Willy's actions and thoughts, particularly his memories, throughout the play. Whenever Willy is unable to accept the present, he retreats to the past, and Biff is usually there. Prior to his Boston trip, Biff adored Willy. He believed his father's stories and accepted his father's philosophy that a person will be successful, provided that he is "well-liked." Biff never questioned Willy, even when it was obvious that Willy was breaking the rules. As a result, Biff grew up believing that he was not bound by social rules or expectations because Willy did not have to abide by them, nor did Willy expect Biff to. It is not surprising that Biff's penchant for stealing continued throughout his adult life because Willy encouraged Biff's "little thefts" while he was growing up. For example, instead of disciplining Biff for stealing the football, Willy praised his initiative.

Biff's perception of Willy as the ideal father is destroyed after Biff's trip to Boston. Once he learns that Willy is having an affair, Biff rejects Willy and his philosophy. Biff considers Willy to be a "fake," and he no longer believes in, or goes along with, Willy's grand fantasies of success. Instead, Biff despises his father and everything he represents.

Biff's problem lies in the fact that, even though he does not want to associate with Willy, he cannot change the fact that he is his son. And as a result, he cannot change the fact that his father has inevitably affected him. It is true that Biff is not a womanizer like his brother Happy, but he has incorporated Willy's tendency to exaggerate and manipulate reality in his favor. For example, Biff truly believes he was a salesman for Oliver, rather than a shipping clerk. It is only when he confronts Oliver that Biff realizes how wrong he was.

Biff is different from Willy because he does finally accept and embrace the fact that he has been living a lie all of his life. Biff is relieved once he realizes who he is and what he wants, as opposed to who Willy thinks he should be and who Biff needs to pretend to be in order to please him. Once Biff states that "We never told the truth for ten minutes in this house," he severs himself from Willy because he openly refuses to live by Willy's philosophy any longer. Ironically, Biff reconciles with Willy almost immediately following this statement. Since he acknowledges that he, too, is a "fake," Biff can no longer hold a grudge against Willy.

Linda Loman

Linda is a woman in an awkward situation. She knows that Willy is suicidal, irrational, and difficult to deal with; however, she goes along with Willy's fantasies in order to protect him from the criticism of others, as well as his own self-criticism. Linda is Willy's champion. She gently prods him when it comes to paying the bills and communicating with Biff, and she does not lose her temper when he becomes irate. Linda knows that Willy is secretly borrowing money from Charley to pay the life insurance and other bills. She has discovered the rubber hose behind the heater and lives in fear that Willy will try to asphyxiate himself. She is also aware that he has attempted to kill himself several times before. Despite all this, Linda does nothing, afraid to aggravate Willy's fragile mental condition. In fact, she even throws Biff and Happy out when their behavior threatens to upset Willy. In many ways Willy is like a small child, and Linda is like a mother who anxiously protects him from Biff, Happy, and the rest of the world.

Linda is a character driven by desperation and fear. Even though Willy is often rude to her and there is the possibility that Linda suspects Willy may have had an affair, she protects him at all costs. According to Linda, Willy is "only a little boat looking for a harbor." She loves Willy, and more importantly, she accepts all of his shortcomings. She would rather play along with his fantasies of grandeur, or the simple ones like building a garden and growing fresh vegetables, than face the possibility of losing him.

Happy Loman

Happy is a young version of Willy. He incorporates his father's habit of manipulating reality in order to create situations that are more favorable to him. Happy grew up listening to Willy embellish the truth, so it is not surprising that Happy exaggerates his position in order to create the illusion of success. Instead of admitting he is an assistant to the assistant, Happy lies and tells everyone he is the assistant buyer. This is Willy's philosophy all over again.

Happy also relishes the fact that "respectable" women cannot resist him. He has seduced the fiancées of three executives just to gain a perception of pleasure and power. He thrives on sexual gratification, but even more than that, Happy savors the knowledge that he has "ruined" women engaged to men he works for and also despises. He states, "I hate myself for it. Because I don't want the girl, and, still, I take it and—I love it!" Happy is similar to Willy in two ways. Both deny their positions and exaggerate details in order to aggrandize themselves, and sexual interludes are the defining moments of both of their lives. Willy's life revolves around his attempt to forget his affair with the Woman, while Happy's life revolves around an active pursuit of affairs with many women.

CRITICAL ESSAYS

On the pages that follow, the writer of this study guide provides critical scholarship on various aspects of Arthur Miller's *Death of a Salesman*. These interpretive essays are intended solely to enhance your understanding of the original literary work; they are supplemental materials and are not to replace your reading of *Death of a Salesman*. When you're finished reading *Death of a Salesman*, and prior to your reading this study guide's critical essays, consider making a bulleted list of what you think are the most important themes and symbols. Write a short paragraph under each bullet explaining *why* you think that theme or symbol is important; include at least one short quote from the original literary work that supports your contention. Then, test your list and reasons against those found in the following essays. Do you include themes and symbols that the study guide author doesn't? If so, this self test might indicate that you are well on your way to understanding original literary work. But if not, perhaps you will need to re-read *Death of a Salesman*.

Miller's Manipulation of Time and Space

Miller often experiments with narrative style and technique. For example, Miller includes lengthy exposition pieces that read as stage directions within *The Crucible*. At first glance, it seems that an audience must either read the information in the program or listen to a long-winded narrator. Upon further inspection however, it becomes apparent that Miller's inclusion of background material allows actors and directors to study character motivation and internalize the information, thereby portraying it in the performance.

Miller provides audiences with a unique experience when it comes to *Death of a Salesman*. In many ways, the play appears traditional. In other words, there are actors who interact with one another, there is a basic plot line, and the play contains standard dramatic elements such as exposition, rising action, conflict, climax, and so forth. However, Miller's manipulation of time and space creates a very non-traditional atmosphere that is unsettling but effective because it mirrors Willy's mental state, thereby allowing the audience to witness his mental instability and take part in it.

Stage directions call for a complete house for the Lomans. An audience will not simply watch the action take place in the kitchen but can observe several rooms within the home. This sounds as if it would be distracting since an audience can view several things at once. After all, what should the audience look at? If more than one character is on stage, whom should the audience pay attention to? Miller solves this problem through lighting. Only characters that are talking or involved in direct action are lit on stage, all other rooms, characters, and props remain in shadow.

The result is a vast number of rooms and props that can be utilized immediately. The audience does not have to wait while a new set is erected or an old one torn down, but instead moves directly and instantaneously into the next scene. Such movement without the benefit of time delays or dialogue transitions produces a disjointed and fragmented sequence of events, much like a dream. In fact, the stage directions in Act I describe the house as follows: "An air of the dream clings to the place, a dream arising out of reality."

Miller does not stop there. Even though the action of the play can shift from one part of the house to another without delay, the action is still limited to the present. Willy's dreams, memories, or recollections of past events must be revealed in a manner that is distinct from actions taking place in the present. This is important for two reasons: First, the audience must be able to differentiate between the present and the past in order to follow the action of the play; second, Willy's increased agitation must be apparent to the audience, and there is no better way to reveal it than to have the audience observe his inability to separate the past from the reality of the present.

Miller achieves this effect by manipulating the space and boundaries of the rooms. When action takes place in the present, characters observe wall boundaries and enter and exit through the doors. During Willy's recollections of the past, characters do not observe wall boundaries, and the action generally takes place in the area at the front of the stage, rather than inside the house. As a result, the audience can distinguish present events from Willy's memories. For example, in Act I, Scene 3, Willy pours a glass of milk in the kitchen, sits down, and begins to mumble to himself. He is in the present. He then remembers a past conversation with the teenage Biff and resumes the conversation. Since this is a past event, Willy directs his speech through the wall to a point offstage. This cues the audience that Willy is digressing in the past.

Sound is also used to create a dreamlike state for both Willy and the audience. A flute melody is associated with Willy, Ben has his own music, laughter cues the Woman, and so forth. Once the sound is introduced with the appropriate character, the audience automatically associates the sound with that same character. As a result, Miller is able to prompt reactions and expectations from the audience, whether they are aware or not. For example, in Act II, Scene 14, it appears that things have finally been settled between Willy and Biff. Even though Biff is leaving in the morning, he and Willy have reconciled. This puts the audience at ease, but once Ben's music is heard, it is evident that the play has not reached its final conclusion. In fact, Ben's appearance may create anxiety for the audience because it suggests an alternate, more disturbing, end to the play.

As the play progresses, the action shifts to the front of the stage. In other words, the audience becomes increasingly aware that the majority of the action is taking place inside Willy's head. It is difficult enough to watch an individual lose his or her identity. It is extremely unsettling and disturbing to be forced to experience the individual's memories, illusions, or perhaps delusions resulting in mental instability. Miller takes that into consideration and then pushes his audiences to the extreme. As Willy's mental state declines, the audience is forced to watch and to react. As a result, the play may be called *Death of a Salesman*, but it is a death observed and experienced by every member of the audience.

Major Themes within *Death of a Salesman*

Death of a Salesman addresses loss of identity and a man's inability to accept change within himself and society. The play is a montage of memories, dreams, confrontations, and arguments, all of which make up the last 24 hours of Willy Loman's life. The three major themes within the play are denial, contradiction, and order versus disorder.

Each member of the Loman family is living in denial or perpetuating a cycle of denial for others. Willy Loman is incapable of accepting the fact that he is a mediocre salesman. Instead Willy strives for his version of the American dream—success and notoriety—even if he is forced to deny reality in order to achieve it. Instead of acknowledging that he is not a well-known success, Willy retreats into the past and chooses to relive past memories and events in which he is perceived as successful.

For example, Willy's favorite memory is of Biff's last football game because Biff vows to make a touchdown just for him. In this scene in the past, Willy can hardly wait to tell the story to his buyers. He considers himself famous as a result of his son's pride in him. Willy's sons, Biff and Happy, adopt Willy's habit of denying or manipulating reality and practice it all of their lives, much to their detriment. It is only at the end of the play that Biff admits he has been a "phony" too, just like Willy. Linda is the only character that recognizes the Loman family lives in denial; however, she goes along with Willy's fantasies in order to preserve his fragile mental state.

The second major theme of the play is contradiction. Throughout the play, Willy's behavior is riddled with inconsistencies. In fact, the only thing consistent about Willy is his inconsistency. From the very beginning of Act I, Scene 1, Willy reveals this tendency. He labels Biff a "lazy bum" but then contradicts himself two lines later when he states, "And such a hard worker. There's one thing about Biff—he's not lazy." Willy's contradictions often confuse audiences at the beginning of the play; however, they soon become a trademark of his character. Willy's inconsistent behavior is the result of his inability to accept reality and his tendency to manipulate or re-create the past in an attempt to escape the present. For example, Willy cannot resign himself to the fact that Biff no longer respects him because of Willy's affair. Rather than admit that their relationship is irreconcilable, Willy retreats to a previous time when Biff admired and respected him. As the play continues, Willy disassociates himself more and more from the present as his problems become too numerous to deal with.

The third major theme of the play, which is order versus disorder, results from Willy's retreats into the past. Each time Willy loses himself in the past, he does so in order to deny the present, especially if the present is too difficult to accept. As the play progresses, Willy spends more and more time in the past as a means of reestablishing order in his life. The more fragmented and disastrous reality becomes, the more necessary it is for Willy to create an alternative reality, even if it requires him to live solely in the past. This is demonstrated immediately after Willy is fired. Ben appears, and Willy confides "nothing's working out. I don't know what to do." Ben quickly shifts the conversation to Alaska and offers Willy a job. Linda appears and convinces Willy that he should stay in sales, just like Dave Singleman. Willy's confidence quickly resurfaces, and he is confident that he has made the right decision by turning down Ben's offer; he is certain he will be a success like Singleman. Thus, Willy's memory has distracted him from the reality of losing his job.

Denial, contradiction, and the quest for order versus disorder comprise the three major themes of *Death of a Salesman*. All three themes work together to create a dreamlike atmosphere in which the audience watches a man's identity and mental stability slip away. The play continues to affect audiences because it allows them to hold a mirror up to themselves. Willy's self-deprecation, sense of failure, and overwhelming regret are emotions that an audience can relate to because everyone has experienced them at one time or another. Individuals continue to react to *Death of a Salesman* because Willy's situation is not unique: He made a mistake—a mistake that irrevocably changed his relationship with the people he loves most—and when all of his attempts to eradicate his mistake fail, he makes one grand attempt to correct the mistake. Willy vehemently denies Biff's claim that they are both common, ordinary people, but ironically, it is the universality of the play which makes it so enduring. Biff's statement, "I'm a dime a dozen, and so are you" is true after all.

CliffsNotes Review

Use this CliffsNotes Review to test your understanding of the original text and reinforce what you've learned in this book. After you work through the review and essay questions, identify the quote section, and the fun and useful practice projects, you're well on your way to understanding a comprehensive and meaningful interpretation of *Death of a Salesman*.

Q&A

1. How does Linda know that Willy is suicidal?

   a. The insurance company informed her that Willy's automobile accidents have been staged.

   b. Willy mentioned suicide to Linda.

   c. Linda found the rubber hose hidden behind the heater.

2. What does Willy want from Howard that makes him go see him?

   a. a recorder

   b. job in New York

   c. a pay raise

3. Who has Willy been borrowing money from?

   a. Howard

   b. Ben

   c. Charley

4. Why does Biff visit Willy in Boston?

   a. Biff wants Willy to come home and convince his teacher to pass him so that he can graduate on time.

   b. He suspects Willy is having an affair. Biff wants to know the truth.

   c. The championship football game is being played in Boston.

5. Why does Happy seduce the fiancées of the young executives he works for?

   a. He is jealous of the young executives and resentful toward them. Seducing their fiancées enables him to get even with them and gain power.

b. Happy has sworn to Linda and Willy that he will get married. He is searching for the right woman.

c. Happy is trying to follow in Willy's footsteps by being involved in illicit affairs.

Answers: (1) c. (2) b. (3) c. (4) a. (5) a.

Identify the Quote: Find Each Quote in *Death of a Salesman*

1. Why, boys, when I was seventeen I walked into the jungle, and when I was twenty-one I walked out. And by God I was rich.

2. You've got to get it into your head now that one day you'll knock on this door and there'll be strange people here.

3. You can't eat the orange and throw the peel away—a man is not a piece of fruit!

4. We never told the truth for ten minutes in this house!

Answers: (1) [Act I, Scene 9: Ben is speaking to Biff and Happy in the past. This quote is important because throughout the play Willy continually refers to Ben's success in Africa, as well as the job Ben offered him in Alaska. Willy equates the Alaskan job opportunity with Ben's African success, and as a result, Willy is convinced that he too would have achieved greatness if he had only taken the job in Alaska. Ben's success symbolizes Willy's own lost opportunity, and a more ideal past.] (2) [Act I, Scene 10: Linda is speaking to Biff. Happy is also present. This quote signals change for the Lomans: All are growing older, Willy's mental health is deteriorating, Willy's livelihood is diminishing, and Biff is changing his ways in order to maintain a relationship at home.] (3) [Act II, Scene 2: Willy is speaking to his boss Howard. This quote symbolizes Willy's entire career and perception of himself. Willy believes he has been discarded now that he is no longer useful. Self-deprecation, along with desperation, compels him to commit suicide.] (4) [Act II, Scene 13: Biff is speaking to Willy. This quote culminates in one of the most climactic confrontations of the play. The entire Loman family is characterized by denial. Willy fails to realize that he manipulates reality. Whenever his memory or perception conflicts with a situation, he simply conforms the situation to his desired reality. Biff's statement is unacceptable and even incomprehensible to Willy because it would force him to deny his own perception of the world and himself.]

Essay Questions

1. Write an essay explaining Willy's philosophy "Be liked and you will never want." How does this statement apply to Willy? To Charley? To Howard? To Bernard?

2. Biff claims he has made every attempt to avoid wasting his life, but he feels like a failure every time he returns home. What type of life or career would make Biff feel successful? Why is he so critical of himself whenever he returns to New York?

3. Compare and contrast Willy's conflicting images of Biff. Why does he defend him and criticize him?

4. Write an essay analyzing Biff's tendency to steal. What compels him to steal? How do his actions shape his future?

5. Explain Happy's obsession with women. Why does he pursue so many women, especially women associated with his employers? How do Happy's affairs relate to Willy's affair?

6. Linda states "life is a casting off." Explain her statement in relation to the play. Who or what is casting off? Or is being cast off? Focus on Willy, Linda, Biff, and Happy.

7. Compare and contrast Willy's death with Dave Singleman's death. What does it mean to die "the death of a salesman" and did Willy achieve that?

8. Think about the significance of Miller's narrative technique. Memories and illusions make up a large portion of the play. How do they affect the play? Consider such things as the story line, character interaction, and overall audience reaction.

Practice Projects

1. Although Miller does not specify what type of salesman Willy is, Miller definitely situates the play in the past. How could you apply Willy's situation to society today? Write a short play in which you give Willy a specific occupation and place it in a modern setting.

2. Construct a scene in which Linda learns of Willy's affair. Concentrate on Linda's reaction to the news, as well as her reactions to Willy and Biff.

CliffsNotes Resource Center

The learning doesn't need to stop here. CliffsNotes Resource Center shows you the best of the best—links to the best information in print and online about the playwright and/or related works. And don't think that this is all we've prepared for you; we've put all kinds of pertinent information at www.cliffsnotes.com. Look for all the terrific resources at your favorite bookstore or local library and on the Internet. When you're online, make your first stop www.cliffsnotes.com where you'll find more incredibly useful information about *Death of a Salesman*.

Books

This CliffsNotes book provides a meaningful interpretation of *Death of a Salesman*. If you are looking for information about the playwright and/or related works, check out these other publications:

The Cambridge Companion to Arthur Miller, edited by Christopher Bigsby. This book provides a chronological overview of Miller's plays and focuses on specific themes within the plays. The chapter on *Death of a Salesman* examines the roles of American myth, consumerism, and denial. The book also addresses Miller's experimentation with dialogue, setting, and linear time within the play. Cambridge: Cambridge University Press, 1997.

Death of a Salesman *and* **The Crucible:** *Text and Performance,* by Bernard F. Dukore. Although this text was published in 1989, it offers a particularly helpful discussion of the importance of stage directions, scenery, lighting, and acting techniques in response to Miller's meticulous stage directions for *Death of a Salesman*. Atlantic Highlands, NJ: Humanities Press International, Inc., 1989.

Timebends, by Arthur Miller. Miller's autobiography describes the process of writing *Death of a Salesman*. Miller discusses his two salesmen uncles, Manny Newman and Lee Balsam, and their influence upon the character Willy Loman. In addition, Miller also reveals the autobiographical aspect of *Death of a Salesman*. New York: Grove Press, 1987.

It's easy to find books published by Wiley Publishing, Inc. You'll find them in your favorite bookstores (on the Internet and at a store near you).

We also have three Web sites that you can use to read about all the books we publish:

■ www.cliffsnotes.com

■ www.dummies.com

■ www.wiley.com

Internet

Check out these Web resources for more information about Arthur Miller and *Death of a Salesman*:

AOL CHAT with Arthur Miller, deathofasalesman.com/aol-chat-miller.htm—This Web page provides a transcript of a chat that took place on February 21, 1999. Miller discusses his views of *Death of a Salesman*, his favorite productions, Willy Loman's role in society today, and other writing projects Miller was working on at the time.

AOL CHAT with Brian Dennehy, deathofasalesman.com/aol-chat-dennehy.htm—This Web page provides a transcript of a chat that took place on February 21, 1999. Dennehy discusses his portrayal of Willy Loman, the challenges of the role, his view of *Death of a Salesman* and its effect on audiences, and the play's connection to Shakespeare.

Arthur Miller's Death of a Salesman, www.deathofasalesman.com—This Web page provides multiple links for both students and teachers. Links include a biography and chronology of events; a complete interview of Miller; reviews of numerous productions; information regarding production techniques, set design, and casting; a suggested reading list; and a comprehensive study guide that includes an analysis of the play, suggested essay topics, and critical thinking exercises.

An Interview with Arthur Miller, www.deathofasalesman.com/am-interview.htm—This Web page provides a transcript of an interview that Matthew C. Roudané conducted in 1985. Miller discusses characterization, language, and the dramatic action of *Death of a Salesman*. In addition, Miller address the relationship between form and content, the role of the American dream motif, parallels to Sophocles, and connections of *Death of a Salesman* to his other works.

Next time you're on the Internet, don't forget to drop by www.cliffsnotes.com. We created an online Resource Center that you can use today, tomorrow, and beyond.

Film

You may find the following film a good production of Miller's play:

Death of a Salesman, Karl Lorimar Home Video, 1986. Directed by Volker Schlondorff and starring Dustin Hoffman, Kate Reid, John Malkovich, Stephen Lang, and Charles Durning. This production of *Death of a Salesman* is unique in that it is filmed on video and therefore is not a live performance in front of an audience; however, the director attempts to retain "play-like" qualities within the movie. For example, rather than create a realistic house for the set, Schlondorff chooses to construct walls and buildings without roofs.

Article

For more information on Arthur Miller and Death of a Salesman, as well as other works by the playwright, check out the following edition of the *Michigan Quarterly Review*:

"A Special Issue: 'Arthur Miller.'" *Michigan Quarterly Review.* Fall 1998. This issue of the *Michigan Quarterly Review* is entirely devoted to Arthur Miller. The issue includes articles on Miller's role within American drama; an article entitled "Willy Loman: Icon of Business Culture," which describes the influence of Willy Loman on the American business community; commentaries on other Miller works; and a series of unpublished photographs of Miller.

Send Us Your Favorite Tips

In your quest for knowledge, have you ever experienced that sublime moment when you figure out a trick that saves time or trouble? Perhaps you realized you were taking ten steps to accomplish something that could have taken two. Or you found a little-known workaround that achieved great results. If you've discovered a useful resource that gave you insight into or helped you understand *Death of a Salesman* and you'd like to share it, the CliffsNotes staff would love to hear from you. Go to our Web site at www.cliffsnotes.com and click the Talk to Us button. If we select your tip, we may publish it as part of CliffsNotes Daily, our exciting, free e-mail newsletter. To find out more or to subscribe to a newsletter, go to www.cliffsnotes.com on the Web.

INDEX

CliffsNotes

LITERATURE NOTES

Absalom, Absalom!
The Aeneid
Agamemnon
Alice in Wonderland
All the King's Men
All the Pretty Horses
All Quiet on the Western Front
All's Well & Merry Wives
American Poets of the 20th Century
American Tragedy
Animal Farm
Anna Karenina
Anthem
Antony and Cleopatra
Aristotle's Ethics
As I Lay Dying
The Assistant
As You Like It
Atlas Shrugged
Autobiography of Ben Franklin
Autobiography of Malcolm X
The Awakening
Babbit
Bartleby & Benito Cereno
The Bean Trees
The Bear
The Bell Jar
Beloved
Beowulf
The Bible
Billy Budd & Typee
Black Boy
Black Like Me
Bleak House
Bless Me, Ultima
The Bluest Eye & Sula
Brave New World
Brothers Karamazov

The Call of the Wild & White Fang
Candide
The Canterbury Tales
Catch-22
Catcher in the Rye
The Chosen
The Color Purple
Comedy of Errors…
Connecticut Yankee
The Contender
The Count of Monte Cristo
Crime and Punishment
The Crucible
Cry, the Beloved Country
Cyrano de Bergerac
Daisy Miller & Turn…Screw
David Copperfield
Death of a Salesman
The Deerslayer
Diary of Anne Frank
Divine Comedy-I. Inferno
Divine Comedy-II. Purgatorio
Divine Comedy-III. Paradiso
Doctor Faustus
Dr. Jekyll and Mr. Hyde
Don Juan
Don Quixote
Dracula
Electra & Medea
Emerson's Essays
Emily Dickinson Poems
Emma
Ethan Frome
The Faerie Queene
Fahrenheit 451
Far from the Madding Crowd
A Farewell to Arms
Farewell to Manzanar
Fathers and Sons
Faulkner's Short Stories

Faust Pt. I & Pt. II
The Federalist
Flowers for Algernon
For Whom the Bell Tolls
The Fountainhead
Frankenstein
The French Lieutenant's Woman
The Giver
Glass Menagerie & Streetcar
Go Down, Moses
The Good Earth
The Grapes of Wrath
Great Expectations
The Great Gatsby
Greek Classics
Gulliver's Travels
Hamlet
The Handmaid's Tale
Hard Times
Heart of Darkness & Secret Sharer
Hemingway's Short Stories
Henry IV Part 1
Henry IV Part 2
Henry V
House Made of Dawn
The House of the Seven Gables
Huckleberry Finn
I Know Why the Caged Bird Sings
Ibsen's Plays I
Ibsen's Plays II
The Idiot
Idylls of the King
The Iliad
Incidents in the Life of a Slave Girl
Inherit the Wind
Invisible Man
Ivanhoe
Jane Eyre
Joseph Andrews
The Joy Luck Club
Jude the Obscure

Julius Caesar
The Jungle
Kafka's Short Stories
Keats & Shelley
The Killer Angels
King Lear
The Kitchen God's Wife
The Last of the Mohicans
Le Morte d'Arthur
Leaves of Grass
Les Miserables
A Lesson Before Dying
Light in August
The Light in the Forest
Lord Jim
Lord of the Flies
The Lord of the Rings
Lost Horizon
Lysistrata & Other Comedies
Macbeth
Madame Bovary
Main Street
The Mayor of Casterbridge
Measure for Measure
The Merchant of Venice
Middlemarch
A Midsummer Night's Dream
The Mill on the Floss
Moby-Dick
Moll Flanders
Mrs. Dalloway
Much Ado About Nothing
My Ántonia
Mythology
Narr. …Frederick Douglass
Native Son
New Testament
Night
1984
Notes from the Underground

Check Out the All-New CliffsNotes Guides

TECHNOLOGY TOPICS

Balancing Your Check-
book with Quicken
Buying and Selling
on eBay
Buying Your First PC
Creating a Winning
PowerPoint 2000
Presentation
Creating Web Pages
with HTML
Creating Your First
Web Page
Exploring the World
with Yahoo!
Getting on the Internet
Going Online with AOL
Making Windows 98
Work for You

Setting Up a
Windows 98
Home Network
Shopping Online Safely
Upgrading and
Repairing Your PC
Using Your First iMac
Using Your First PC
Writing Your First
Computer Program

PERSONAL FINANCE TOPICS

Budgeting & Saving
Your Money
Getting a Loan
Getting Out of Debt
Investing for the
First Time
Investing in
401(k) Plans
Investing in IRAs
Investing in
Mutual Funds
Investing in the
Stock Market
Managing Your Money
Planning Your
Retirement
Understanding
Health Insurance
Understanding
Life Insurance

CAREER TOPICS

Delivering a Winning
Job Interview
Finding a Job
on the Web
Getting a Job
Writing a Great Resume